Three Plays of Euripides

Three Plays of Euripides

Alcestis
Medea
The Bacchae

Translated by
Paul Roche

W·W·NORTON & COMPANY·INC·New York

Copyright © 1974 by Paul Roche

FIRST EDITION

Library of Congress Cataloging in Publication Data
Euripides.
    Three plays of Euripides.
    I. Roche, Paul, 1927–   tr.   II. Title.
PA3975.A2   1974   882'.01   73–13587
ISBN 0–393–04382–7

Published simultaneously in Canada
by George J. McLeod Limited, Toronto

PRINTED IN THE UNITED STATES OF AMERICA

1 2 3 4 5 6 7 8 9 0

Contents

C 5

For Mary Roche Geoghegan

Vos exemplaria Graeca
Nocturna versate manu, versate diurna.

—Horace, *Ars Poetica*

(For yourselves you thumb well,
by night and day, Greek models.)

Introduction

The Mighty Themes of Euripides

To put it most baldly, one might say that what Euripides wrote about was war, women, and God. Sadly for Euripides, however, none of these mighty themes made him popular, for he was too intense an individualist to compromise and too comprehensive a soul to accommodate himself to narrow-mindedness.

His onslaughts on war came at a time when Athens was locked in her twenty-seven-year useless and extravagant death-struggle with Sparta—another Vietnam if ever there was one. Euripides' indictment of the sheer wastefulness and stupidity of war must have seemed to many of his contemporaries nothing but crass lack of patriotism.

As to women, Euripides was obsessed with their plight. Out of his nineteen extant plays no fewer than twelve are about women. Although he does not always portray them in the best of colors, he is so much in their favor that at least two of his tragedies, *Medea* and *Alcestis*, are propaganda tracts for women's liberation. Moreover, when one of his women turns sour, be it a Medea or a Phaedra, it is because her man has let her down. And when one of Euripides' women turns sour, she turns savage, is eaten up with the passion to get even with her man and is driven to an animal fury that is all too human.

Of Euripides' third theme, God (and the gods), it must be said at once that all Greek tragedy is ultimately theological; that is, it is about the relationship of man to fellow man in an environment which makes no sense unless it includes the recognition of powers greater than man's. With religious ideas far in advance of those of their time, the great Greek dramatists Aeschylus, Sophocles, and Euripides wanted to get men away from their puny concept of the gods as simply bigger human beings acting out the human scene at an Olympian level. Aeschylus and Sophocles tried to shift their contemporaries to an idea of God based on something more than a primitive and vindictive tribal Zeus. Euripides went further. He showed that any other stance was absurd and unworthy of mortals. "You say these so-called deities are immortal and omnipotent. I'll make you see they are nothing more than a set of self-canceling, willful, lustful, tantrum-prone children. . . . Look into your own souls if you want to find where true destiny and godhead lie." Such was the purport of his message. He was branded an atheist.

It is hardly surprising, given the masses' resistance to change in any age, that Euripides, the Ibsen and Shaw of his, was resisted. Even Aristophanes made fun of him. In spite of the bewitching beauty of his words and the theatrical brilliance of his characters, effects to which the Athenians were by no means immune, he was accorded the prize for tragedy only four times in his life, whereas Sophocles received it eighteen and Aeschylus thirteen. Even his *Medea*, perhaps his masterpiece after *The Bacchae*, won only third place. Disappointment and lack of recognition may well have been the reason for his leaving Athens in self-appointed exile and going to live at the court of the king of Macedon.

But neither is it surprising that when the new ideas did begin to take root, Euripides became more popular than Aeschylus and Sophocles put together. And his popularity lasted.[1] This belated acceptance was probably helped by the generous gesture of Sophocles, Euripides' senior by some seventeen years and his lifelong rival, who on hearing of Euripides' death (and himself an old man nearing ninety), is said to have brought on his chorus at the festival dressed in mourning. The Athenians themselves, a year or so later, recognizing the caliber of the poet they had lost, awarded him the prize for the fifth time when *The Bacchae* was first performed in Athens.

This horror story of disconcerting beauty was written at a turning point of history—the eve of the collapse of Athens. It examines in mythical form the whole attitude of man toward religion and reason, the conscious and unconscious mind, and the concepts of freedom and beauty when these are pitted against the psychology of orthodoxy and expediency. The play shows that there exists a dark underside to life, shrouding more than the mind can know. To war against it is to war against the elemental in one's own nature and to cut oneself off from primary knowledge—that accumulation of primitive experience which goes to make a human being. To put oneself in tune with it is to put oneself in touch with a luminous though unfathomable whole.

Dionysus here is not the rollicking, jolly god popularized by the Romans, but the dangerous embodiment of the life force itself, one whose radiant presence cannot be bound by chains and the prison cell, and whose ineluctable impact draws men to their release, glory, or destruction. "To resist Dionysus is to repress the elemental . . ."

---

1. After the death of Alexander the Great, when Greek theaters and Greek culture spread over the world, Euripides was played everywhere. In 53 B.C., just after the crushing defeat of the Roman army at Carrhae under Crassus (the multimillionaire who had bought himself a generalship), *The Bacchae* was actually being performed at the Parthian court, and Crassus' head was rushed to the theater in time to be mounted on top of Agave's bloody thyrsus. So they say.

and to hasten that "sudden collapse of the inward dykes when the elemental breaks through perforce and civilization vanishes."[2] We must learn what it costs to abuse something profound and holy.

To my mind, *The Bacchae* is one of the greatest plays ever written. It never loses its layers of significance. To the Greeks of the fifth century B.C. and to every age succeeding them, it points in many directions and is full of warning. Progress and reason must be balanced with something deeper, some subliminal wholeness. Those who divorce themselves from the vibrant potency of nature are the very ones in greatest danger of losing their reason, which is the control that keeps the supernatural in its context precisely by recognizing it.

I have chosen these plays to translate because all three, though in different ways and to different degrees, air Euripides' main themes. All three are perfect examples of his range, manner, and style.[3] All three are exhibitions of Euripides' grasp of individual psychology and his ability to depict actual life rather than idealizations of life (as with Aeschylus and Sophocles). And finally, all three contain strong elements of his humor. It was Euripides' handling of humor, with its tragicomic realism, which inspired the New Comedy in the succeeding century and gave birth to melodrama and the comedy of manners.

Notes of a Translator

Translations, it has been said, are like wives: the beautiful are seldom faithful, and the faithful are seldom beautiful. Yet poets and scholars, lured by the discipline of an impossible challenge, continue to attempt the perfect match: a translation at once totally faithful and totally beautiful. Few readers realize by what a slender thread the truth of a great work hangs, or how enormous is the responsibility of the translator.

The problem is primarily poetic, or at least as much poetic as semantic; for what has to be achieved is not simply a transference of meanings but a transposition of sounds. It is in the amazing complex of rhythm, cadence, and tone that the feelings of a language are locked. Since these are untransferable, a new system of rhythms, cadences, and tones has to be invented which will get as near as possible to those expressed in the original. The translator wants his translation to sound as if it had been written in his own

2. Euripides, *The Bacchae*, ed. E. R. Dodds (Oxford: Clarendon Press, 1966), p. xvi.
3. The form of *The Bacchae* is for Euripides unique. Late play though it is, he goes back to a very old form: the form of choral lyric as used by Aeschylus.

tongue, and yet he is in a straitjacket. He must not make up what is not there; he must hew to the meaning of what is given; and he must as far as possible bring over, too, the style and form. The listener wants to know not merely what the great poet said but how he said it.

My own principles, after a long apprenticeship with no fewer than thirteen Greek and Latin plays, may seem obvious, but to put them into practice is not so simple. Nevertheless, these have been my guiding lights:

1. One language best translates another when it is truest to its own genius and tries not to imitate but to recreate.
2. In attempting to reproduce the style and form of the original, the second language must aim not at identification but at the esthetic equivalent.
3. When all else is right but pace is not right, nothing is right.

To take the last point first, the important thing to remember in Greek drama is that the verbal pace is fast—much faster than many translators will allow. I wondered why this was true when I first read aloud the opening lines of *Antigone* some eighteen years ago and compared them to one of the most widely accepted translations then current. Both used lines of twelve syllables, both were in iambic hexameter (that is what theoretically seemed in English to be nearest to the iambic trimeter of the Greek), and yet the difference in pace was enormous. What made the English so much slower? Then I noticed that English uses almost twice as many consonants. It is the consonants that delay. One has only to take a two-syllable Greek word like *sophos* and compare it to a two-syllable word in English like *knowledge* to see how even in one word the difference is ummistakable. When this difference is multiplied by many words in a line, many lines on a page, the slowing-up process can be deadening.

To implement my second principle, that in trying to reproduce the style and form of the original, the second language must aim not at identification but at the esthetic equivalent, I adopted what I call "The Freewheeling Iambic," a line that expands and contracts at will, following the contours of the voice. This I have found is the best I can do to get anywhere near the mobility of the Greek: its extraordinary fluidity which somehow performs the miracle of being spontaneous and formal in the same breath. This is the line I now use in all my translations.

Thirdly and lastly: One language best translates another when it is truest to its own genius and tries not to imitate but to recreate. One language cannot take a photograph of another; it can only make a painting. Imitation Greek is not Greek and only bad English. But there is another kind of fidelity which is real. It depends on watching the two languages with a hawk's eye and a mouse's ear, transposing those qualities of sound that are common to both tongues. For Greek and English, though different in their genius, share many predilections. The poet-translator must keep his eyes and ears on both, never imitating the one but seizing every chance of a parallel effect in the other.

To give an example, I shall take a phrase from the poet Horace: "Quidquid dicam aut erit aut non," which, word for word, translates as: "Whatever I may say will either be or not be." Alas, where has gone the aphoristic humor of the Latin? There is nothing clever or funny about the deadbeat English. So I begin to repeat over and over to myself the rhythm of the Latin. At last I come out with: "Whatever I may say will certainly be, or certainly not." Yes, this begins to get near it. I have not translated the *aut . . . aut* ("either . . . or") at all, but have caught the emphasis of the repetition by the English "certainly . . . certainly"; what is more, I am pitched into the sudden, full stop of the "not" exactly in the same way as Horace pitches you into his sudden *non*.

And now a word about rhyme. Scholars will solemnly tell you there is no rhyme in Greek poetry. This is not true. There are many examples of rhyme even in tragedy. The point is that a rhyme at the end of a long polysyllabic word gets less emphasis than it would in English and therefore goes undetected. But it is there and has its effect. Moreover, the internal chiming that goes on in a passage of Greek poetry is so rich in assonance, consonance, and slant rhyme, that to adopt full rhymes at the ends of words would be to overdo it. Therefore, I use rhyme sparsely. But I do use it, because it is very much part of the tradition of English and helps to recapture the richness of the Greek.

Which brings me to a final plea. Greek tragedy operates through the ear. It is through the ear primarily that it enters the eyes, the senses, the mind, the heart. It must be spoken aloud. It is designed for that. And until that is done these plays have not been read, have not been used, have not been born.

Textual Note

The texts I have used in making these translations are the following:

Medea: that edited by Professor Denys L. Page (Oxford: Clarendon Press, 1967); and also that set out in The Loeb Classical Library based on an edition by Gilbert Murray.

Alcestis: The Loeb Classical Library.

The Bacchae: that edited by E. R. Dodds (Oxford: Clarendon Press, 1966).

The line numbers in the right-hand margins refer to the line numbers of the Greek original, not to my translations. This is intended to make it easier for readers to compare my translations with the original.

PAUL ROCHE
CALIFORNIA INSTITUTE OF THE ARTS
MAY 1973

Three Plays of Euripides

Alcestis

Characters

APOLLO
DEATH
CHORUS, *elders of Pherae*
MAID
ALCESTIS, *wife of Admetus*
ADMETUS, *king of Pherae*
EUMELUS, *son of Admetus and Alcestis*
HERACLES
PHERES, *father of Admetus*
BUTLER
ATTENDANTS, *guards, maids, mourners*

Time and Setting

The god Apollo, *constrained by his father to tend the cattle of Admetus, king of Pherae in Thessaly, finds the king a just and hospitable master, and to reward him he extracts from the Fates[1] the promise that Admetus will be let off death when his time comes, provided someone else dies for him. No one can be found except his own wife, Alcestis. Admetus accepts the sacrifice but with the passing years comes to realize what a perfect wife Alcestis is and that without her life will be intolerable. There is no way, however, to recall an arrangement made with the implacable Fates.*

And now at last the fatal day has come: the queen is dying. People anxiously ask, "Is there no hope?" Apollo arrives to plead with Death for Alcestis' life. Splendidly dressed as an archer, with bow and quiver, he steps into the city square of Pherae outside the palace.

Prologue

APOLLO
    The house of Admetus
and I a lowly servant here
—I a god—and all because
Zeus slew my son Asclepius:
hurled lightning through his heart.
In my rage I killed his Cyclopes,[2]   5

---

1. *Fates*: powerful goddesses who presided over the birth, life, and death of all humans. They were three sisters, the youngest of whom, Clotho, presided over the moment of birth. Lachesis spun out the thread of life, and Atropos, the eldest, cut the thread of human life with scissors.
2. *Cyclopes*: a race of giants whose characteristic feaure was their single eye in the center of their foreheads. They inhabited the western part of Sicily, were characteristically uncivilized, and had been employed in making armor and weapons for the gods under the direction of Hephestus, whom the Latins called Vulcan. When Zeus (Latin name *Jupiter* or *Jove*) punished Asclepius (son of Apollo and Coronis, a Lapith princess) for raising the dead to life, and killed

1

who forge his thunderbolts, and for my punishment
the Father made me flunky to mere mortal man.
   So, here I came, this host's cattleman,
and upholder of his house until this day.
Yes, upright myself, I found an upright man,   10
so I snatched him from his time of death,
I tricked the Fates.
   Those ladies made this bargain with me:
"We'll let Admetus off his dying, for now,
if he'll exchange one body for another down below."
   Well, he canvassed and solicited   15
all his near and dear:
father, old gray-haired mother,
and found absolutely no one
to give up the light for him and die;
no one, that is, except his wife.
   She's limp in his arms this moment in the house,
gasping out her last.   20
Today's the day she has to die and flit from life.
   But I am leaving.
I don't want Death smeared over me,
though I've come to love this friendly house.
      [*he sees* DEATH *emerge from behind a pillar, drably and*
      lugubriously dressed, with a drawn sword.]
   There's Death himself, the great undertaker
all prepared to take her down to the house of hell,   25
right on time: he's been watching for this date—
the day she has to die.
DEATH [*stepping back with a snarl*]
   What are you doing here, you Apollo, in this city—
prowling about outside the palace?
   Up to no good again, eh?
Purloining the privileges of the powers below,   30
filching their perquisites
   Weren't you satisfied with undoing
Admetus's dying—
tricking the Fates with a lowdown trick?
   Now you protect with quiver and bow
this daughter of Pelias,[3] and his wife,   35
though it was all agreed that she
should lose her own to save his life.

---

him with a thunderbolt. Apollo retaliated
by massacring Zeus' Cyclopes (see lines
124–30).

3. *Pelias*: Usurper of the kingdom of Iolcus, he sent Jason to get the Golden
Fleece. His daughters were called the
Peliades, of whom Alcestis was one. She,
together with her sisters, had been
tricked by Medea into chopping up her
father and boiling the pieces in order to

magically restore him to youth. The ex-
periment failed, and the Peliades fled to
Corinth, where Admetus took them in.
He married Alcestis, but when her
brother brought an army against Admetus and took him prisoner, he was able
to save his life only by finding another
to take his place. Alcestis was the only
one who offered to do this, and Admetus
accepted.

APOLLO. I've got my reasons: fair ones too.
DEATH. Fair ones? With a bow and arrow?
APOLLO. You know I always carry these.   40
DEATH. To give this house illegal help, eh?
APOLLO. No . . . But I am sad to see my friend in trouble.
DEATH. So you'd wrest this second body from me too?
APOLLO. I never wrested what you call the first.
DEATH. Then why is *he* on earth, not underneath?   45
APOLLO. Because the wife you've come for ransomed him.
DEATH. Exactly so. And soon I'll have her under sods.
APOLLO. Take her, then, and go . . . I can't dissuade you, I suppose.
DEATH. From killing, when I must? Why, that's my work.
APOLLO. Your work should be to carry off the ripe.   50
DEATH. I see what you're leading up to with such warmth.
APOLLO. If only Alcestis could attain old age!
DEATH. Certainly not. I enjoy my rights as well, you know.
APOLLO. The life you take, soon or later, won't be more than one.
DEATH. Young deaths are more valuable.   55
APOLLO. Old deaths have the richer funerals.
DEATH. Tut tut, Apollo! Always legislating for the rich?
APOLLO. How disingenuous! And how *naïve*!
DEATH. Who would not buy Death off until old age?
APOLLO. So you won't oblige me with this little favor?   60
DEATH. Of course not. Don't you understand my principles?
APOLLO. Yes: hateful to human beings, distasteful to the gods.
DEATH. You can't just suit yourself in everything, you know.
APOLLO. I'll tell you something, Death:
    ruthless as you are, you will be stopped.
        A man is coming to this house of Pheres,   65
    a hero sent by Eurýstheus[4]
    to fetch a team of horses from the wintry plains of Thrace.
        He'll be a welcome guest in this palace of Admetus,
    and he'll take that woman from you forcibly.
        You'll have no thanks from me in this, just my dislike.   70
    and yet you'll do it.
        [APOLLO *strides away*]
DEATH. Mouth away. It'll do no good.
        This woman *shall* go down to Hades.
        I'm approaching now,
    my sword is at the ready.
        Every head of hair this blade has shorn
    is dedicated to the nether gods forlorn.   75
        [DEATH *slinks away*]
        [*enter the* CHORUS, *the old men of Pherae. They divide
        into several groups and chant back and forth to each other*]

---

4. *Eurýstheus*: a king of Argos and My-
cenae, who was so jealous of the fame
of Heracles, his younger cousin, that he
sent him on the dangerous enterprises
known as the Twelve Labors of Heracles (Latin name of Heracles: *Hercules*).

PARODOS OR ENTRY SONG

CHORUS

1: What is this hush before the palace?
   Why is Admetus' house so quiet?
   There is no friend at hand to tell us   80
   Whether we ought to weep for our queen
   As dead, or whether our lady yet
   Lives and looks upon the light:
   Alcestis, child of Pelias—
   Who seems to me and all of us
   The best of wives a man could get.   85

2: Can you hear a keening note—   [Strophe 1]
   Beating of hands inside the home?
   Or solemn wail of requiem?
   No one stands outside the gate.   90
   O come, Apollo, through the foam
           Of seething woe
               And Fate.
3: They'd not be silent if she'd passed.
4: She's dead and cold.
3: No cortege yet has left the house.   95
4: How do you know? I wish I had your hope.
3: Would Admetus have denied
   His noble bride
   The proper pomp?

1: Nor do I see outside   [Antistrophe 1] 100
   The vase of water from a spring,
   The lustral offering
   Put beside
   The front door of the dead.
   Or the clipped tresses in the hall
   Which the mourners should make fall
   Or the beating hands of girls.   105
2: Yet this is the fatal day . . .
3: Can you be sure?
2: On which it is decreed for her
   To pass away, down below.
3: You break my heart, you bruise my soul.
1: When the best of us so fade
   The longest loyal
   Mourn in the shade.   110

2: There is no place to sail: [Strophe 2]
   Lycía or the vale   115
   Of rainless Ammon⁵ where
   We could loose the soul

5. *Ammon*: a name for Zeus, a temple for whom stands in the Libyan desert.

Of this dying girl.
3: The cliff of doom is sheer.
   What altars shall I near   120
   Or sacrifice prepare?
   What god could hear my prayer?

4: Apollo's son alone   [*Antistrophe* 2]
   Were he alive again   125
   Could make her leave the gloom
   And portals of the night
   To come into the light.
   1: For he could raise the dead
      Before the lightning sped
      And seared him to his end
      But now what hope is left
      For a life bereft?   130
   2: Admetus has performed
      All the rites he can:
      All the altars fume
      With sacrifice and none
      Can bring the slightest balm.
      [*a* MAID *has entered*]
LEADER. Look, here comes a woman from the palace,   135
   a servant maid in tears . . . What shall we be told?
   Has something happened to my Lord and Lady?
   Then we shall mourn. But we must know.
   Is our mistress still alive, or is she dead?   140

First Episode

MAID. You might say she is living and she's dying.
LEADER. Seeing and deceased? it makes no sense.
MAID. She's sinking now: breathing out her last.
LEADER. Poor Master, losing such a lovely mistress!
MAID. And not to feel the shock of it until it's struck.   145
LEADER. Is all hope gone of saving her?
MAID. Her hour has come: there's no avoiding it.
LEADER. What! Even to the final obsequies?
MAID. Yes, everything: the funeral is arranged.
LEADER. What a noble way to go!
   the best wife ever under heaven.   150
MAID. The best of course. Who would deny it?
   What paragon could hope surpass her?
   How could a woman show
more devotion to her man than die for him?   155
   All this is common knowledge in the world outside.
   Wait till you hear how she behaved at home.
   The moment that she knew her final day had come,
she bathed her milk-white body in water from the river,

chose from the cedar chests her jewels and best apparel,   160
decked herself out handsomely;
then stood before the hearth and made this prayer.
    "Hesta, lady,
On my way down to the dark,
This last time I kneel to you and pray:
Be a mother to my little ones.   165
Give my son a loving bride,
An upright husband to my daughter.
Keep them from an early death
—not like their mother's—
And round them out a happy lot
Living in their native land."
Then she went to every altar in Admetus' halls,   170
hung them with wreaths and prayed,
offering sprigs of myrtle[6]
she broke off from a branch.
    There was no sighing or sobbing.
    The doom she walked towards
did not even dim the sweet tenor of her face.
    Then to her room she flew and to the bed,   175
and there the tears began.
    "Bed, my bed," she cried,
    "where I unlocked my maidenhood
for this very-man for whom today I die: farewell.
I do not hate you—see—
though you caused my death . . . but only mine.
I would not fail you, or my man, and so I die.   180
Some other bride will own you soon:
not more chaste than I, but happier perhaps."
    Falling on the bed, she kissed it
and let the flood of tears that swept her eyes
bestrew the coverlet
    And when she had wept her fill   185
she tottered from the bed, all limp,
wandered away and back again, many times,
throwing herself upon the bed.
    Meanwhile, the little children sobbed,
clinging to their mother's skirts.
    She took them each in turn,   190
hugged and fondled them
like one about to die.
    And all the women in the house were crying
in pity for their lady mistress.
    She held out her hand to each:
none too low for her to greet   195
and wait for her reply.

6. *Myrtle*: a very different plant from the   *myrtle* in America.
periwinkle, which has come to be called

These are the sad things happening now
inside Admetus' home.
  If *he* had died,
it had been over and done with.
  As it is, his escape
has brought on him such pain he never will forget.
LEADER. He must be calling out in anguish
  at the loss of such a wife.   200
MAID. Yes, he holds his loved one in his arms
  and weeps and says:
    "Do not desert me. Do not desert me,"
  asking the impossible;
  for she wilts, she droops in her decline.
    Yet, upright still, scarcely able to draw breath, 205
  she trails her hand as if it were a weight,
  wishing still to face the sun
  and let her eyes go feasting on its rays
  one last time.
    [*the* MAID *pauses and surveys the dismal looks of the old
    men.*]
  I'll go in now and say that you are here.
Such concern and loyalty is rare: 210
to rally to the great ones in their need.
But you have been my Lord and Lady's friend for many a year.
    [*exit* MAID]
    [*several groups of the* CHORUS *chant successively, hoping
    against hope that there may still be a way to save* ALCESTIS]
  1: What escape, O Zeus, is there
      For our sovereign from despair?
  2: What smallest chink of hope is left?
      Or must I tear my hair?   215
      Put on a mourning dress?
  3: Friends, it's clearly all too clear
      But let us offer prayer:
      The gods have power.
ALL. Lord Apollo, healer,   220
      Find a way to help Admetus.
  1: Procure—provide—a plan.
      You always did, we know you can.
      Snatch her from Death's door
      Keep murderous Hades back.   225
  4: Son of Pheres, overwhelming
      Will you find your consort's going:
      The lack! The lack!
  2: Enough to make a person loose
      His very life with knife or noose.   230
  3: O his loved one, his belovéd,
      He today will see her dead!

1: Look, she comes, she comes
    With her husband from her home.
ALL. Wail it out, shout it in groans, O land of Pherae:
        The perfect woman   235
        Sick and sinking now towards the world of Hades!
        Without a doubt a wedding makes
    Much more pain than joy. Look at the past
        And now at the sufferings of our king: 240
        Bereft of his wife, his nonpareil,
            He will live
        An unlivable life of gray.
    [*the doors of the palace open and* ALCESTIS, *half carried by*
    ADMETUS, *walks down the steps. The little boy* EUMELUS *and*
    his sister cling to their mother. The servants set up a couch as
    ALCESTIS *and* ADMETUS *chant to each other.*]
ALCESTIS. The sun and the day's clear light,
    The clouds in the wheeling sky . . .   245
ADMETUS. Have us two unhappy beings in sight.
    We did the gods no wrong that you should die.
ALCESTIS. The sweet earth and this lovely home
    And the land I came from as a bride . . .
ADMETUS. Bear up, my darling. Do not leave me alone.   250
    Ask, and the mighty gods may not turn aside.
ALCESTIS. I see the boat with its brace of oarblades
    —the ferry of corpses—
    And resting his arm on an oar,
    Charon is calling.
    "Quick, get aboard, you waste my time,"   255
    He harasses, he hurries me to come.
ADMETUS. Oh, what a bitter passage you envisage!
    Our pain, my woebegotten one, is savage.
ALCESTIS. I am dragged, oh, dragged, to the court of the dead: 260
    Cannot you see?
    His eyes are grim and they glower on me.
    He is winged. He is Hades.
    What? . . . No, no! Let me go . . . Ah, this going
    Is utterly bleak . . . Yes, I'm coming.
ADMETUS. He wrenches at the heart of those who love you: 265
    Me most of all, but all of those who have you.
ALCESTIS [*trying to disengage herself*]
    Let me go. Let me go. I am ready.
    My legs give way . . .
    Put me down . . . for Hades
    Is on me.
    Over my eyes a film of darkness
    Creeps; O my children, my babies,   270
    You are motherless now, but you must bless
    The light still good to see.
ADMETUS. These are the heaviest words to hear.

Worse than death are these words to me.
By the gods, do not leave me, I beg, don't dare,   275
For the sake of the children you hold dear.
Look up and resist.
Once you are gone, I no longer exist:
In you we are not, or in you we are.
For you are the love we adore.
    [ADMETUS *gently walks* ALCESTIS *to the couch and lays her*
    down. She takes his hand]
ALCESTIS. Admetus, you can see how matters stand with me,   280
so let me tell you my last wish before I die.
    I have cherished you
and though it cost me my own life
set your eyes to gaze upon this sunlight still.
    I die for you, though had I wished   285
I could have wed again, and made a prosperous royal home.
    But I had no wish to live apart from you
and with these children orphaned,
even though it meant the sacrifice of youth and all its gifts
—which I so enjoyed—
and even though your own father   290
and the mother who gave you birth,
who were ripe enough to die with grace
—yes, die gracefully and praised—
for their own son's sake, abandoned you . . .
an only son at that,
with no prospect of a further heir when you were gone.   295
    We could have lived our days out to the end,
you and I, and you no weeping widower
with children who were motherless.
    Well, some destiny has arranged things as they are,
so be it, but remember always what you owe to me:
something I can never ask you to repay,   300
for nothing is so valuable as life—
as you yourself will readily admit.
    [*she turns her head and rests her eyes on the two children,*
    who stand by with their nurse]
These children you will love no less than I
if your heart be right;
so bring them up as masters in my home.
    Do not remarry and impose on them   305
some vicious stepmother who through jealousy of me
takes her hand to them—
these your little ones and also mine.
    Do not do that, I beg you—Oh, not that!—
a second wife
loathes the children there before she came . . .
Is about as tender as an adder.   310

    A boy's great bulwark is his father:

he goes to him and waits on his advice;
but a girl, you, my little daughter,
what kind of girlhood can you have?
What kind of woman would you find your father's second wife?
   Not one, I only hope,
who blasts your maiden prime away with vicious gossip   315
and blights your wedding day.
   There'll be no mother at your wedding
to see you through,
and none to cheer you at your lying-in,
just when a mother is so comforting.
   Yes, I must die,   320
and not tomorrow or the following day:
the great ordeal is now;
in a moment I'll be reckoned with the ones who passed away.
   Farewell. Be happy.
   You, my husband, can be proud,
you married such a wife as I; and you, my children,
to have had me as your mother.   325
LEADER. Madam, be consoled. I do not hesitate to speak for him:
all this he'll do—or else be raving mad.
   [ADMETUS *kneels beside his wife and presses her hand*]
ADMETUS. It shall be as you say,
exactly as you say. Have no fear.
   As in life you alone were mine,
so in death no one else
shall be called my wife.   330
   No Thessalian bride shall ever claim me after you.
   None is so nobly born,
none so beautiful—not one.
   As for children, I have no need of more.
   May ours bring some joy to me,
seeing all joy in you is dead.   335
   I shall weep for you—
not just one year
but as long as life shall last;
yes, my love, forever.
   And her who gave me birth I'll hate, and curse my father.
   Their love was only words; but you, you gave
the most precious thing you had to save my life.   340
   The loss—the loss of one like you—
how can I not cry out in pain?
   [*he turns toward the citizens*]
   All celebrations I disallow, all drinking parties:
no more song and garlands in my house;
no more music from the lyre—not one chord—   345
I'll sing no ditty to the flute.
   For you, you take my heart away with you.
   I'll have some craftsman fashion

an effigy of you
and lay it sleeping in my bed.
I'll fall on it and fondle it,   350
calling out your name   ·
and think I have my darling in my arms
whom I have not.
    Cold comfort, certainly,
but still a way of lessening the load upon my soul.
    In dreams perhaps you'll come to me and make me glad: 355
it's sweet to see our loved ones, even in the night,
even for the moment that they last.
    If I had the tongue of Orpheus
and his mellifluous tunes
and by my song could cast a spell
on Persephone and her spouse
and wrest you out of hell,
I should go down,
and neither Pluto's hound   360
nor spirit-carrying Charon[7] at his oar
could stop me till I'd brought your soul
up into the light.
    But, wait for me down there: wait for me to die.
Prepare the home where you and I shall live as one.
    For I shall make them lay my bones   365
side by side with yours,
stretched out with you
in the selfsame cedar box.
    No, not even in death,
would I be apart from you:
my one, my only faithful love.
LEADER. We too shall share, as friend with friend,
    your heaving grief for her. That much is right.   370
       [ALCESTIS *raises herself a little and beckons the two chil-*
       dren to her side]
ALCESTIS. Children, you have heard your father's promise:
    never to marry again at your expense and my dishonor.
ADMETUS. Yes, I say it now and *shall* do as I say.
ALCESTIS [*taking the children's hands*]
    On these terms, then, take the children from my hand.   375
ADMETUS. I do. A lovely present from a hand so loved.
ALCESTIS. Be these children's mother now instead of me.
ADMETUS. [*holding the children's hands*]
    Everything constrains me now they don't have you.
ALCESTIS. Dear children, I must leave you
    when I should be most alive.
ADMETUS. And me? What am I to do   380
    when I am left and you are gone.

7. *Charon*: he who ferries the dead   the realm of Hades.
across the Rivers Styx and Acheron to

ALCESTIS. Time will heal you. And the dead are nothing.
ADMETUS. By all the gods then, take me with you.
Take me down below.
ALCESTIS. No: my dying is enough—my dying for you.
ADMETUS. O Death, what a consort you would rob me of!
ALCESTIS. [*sinking back*] My eyes . . . so heavy now . . . weighted
with the dark.   385
ADMETUS. Wife, my wife, you leave me—leave me lost.
ALCESTIS. Say I am nothing, then: no longer here.
ADMETUS. Lift up your head. Will you let your children go?
ALCESTIS. I must, against my will. Goodbye, my little ones.
ADMETUS. Look at them, look up.   390
ALCESTIS. I am nothing now.
ADMETUS. What? . . . Are you slipping from us?
ALCESTIS. Farewell.
        [ALCESTIS, *still in* ADMETUS' *arms, falls back dead*]
ADMETUS. I am most miserable and lost.
LEADER. She is gone. Admetus' wife is no more.
EUMELUS. [*tearing from his nurse and throwing himself on his
        dead mother*] Oh . . . !   [*Strophe*]

My mother's gone now
Down below
She's no longer in the sun.   395
Father, she has left, poor Mummy,
Now I live without a mother.
Look, her eyelids; look, her fingers:
They are limp now.
Listen, Mother, listen to me.   400
Yes, it's me. Oh, Mummy, me.
Your little chick is calling, falling
As he used to
On your lips.
ADMETUS [*gently disengaging him*]
She can't see you, she can't hear you.
You and I are weighted under   405
By the heaviest fate.

EUMELUS. But, Father, I'm too little   [*Antistrophe*]
To find myself alone.
Mummy's gone and, oh,
Everything is horrid.
You, my little sister,   410
know this sadness too.
It is awful, Father, awful:
Your marriage never lasted
Till old age with her.
She has gone before you
And, Mother, now without you
Our home is over.   415

LEADER. Admetus, you must bear
  this catastrophe.
    You're not the first and not the last
  to lose a noble wife.
    Acknowledge
  that all of us must pay the debt of death.
ADMETUS. I admit it,
  nor did this evil swoop without a warning: 420
  it has tormented me for long.
    [*he rises slowly from* ALCESTIS' *couch*]
  Well . . . I shall arrange the cortege for the dead.
  You stay here and chant the dirge
  to the god who is implacable.
    Every Thessalian in my realm,   425
  draped in black, with shaven head,
  I ask to join in mourning for this lady.
    You grooms who harness
  both single horse and chariot-in-four,
  see all manes are sheared.
    And let there be throughout the city   430
  no sound of pipe or lyre
  till full twelve moons have run their course.
    Never shall I put beneath the sod
  a more beloved or more generous friend.
    Rightly I salute her, for she died—and she alone—
  in my stead.
    [*the servants and attendants gather up the body of* ALCESTIS
    to prepare it for burial]

FIRST CHORAL ODE

1: Child of Pelias   [*Strophe* 1   435
    I wave you my farewell towards the palace
    And sunless house of Hades, there to dwell.
2: Let Hades understand, that god of midnight hair,
    And that antique and grisly man   440
    Who sits and steers
    The ferry for the dead
    That he has sped
    In his skiff of double oars   445
    By far, by far
    The most excelling wife of all.

3: Much shall the music-makers   [*Antistrophe* 1]
    On the mountain tortoise shell
    Be your celebrators
    And sing to the seven-stringed
    Lyre, or without it sing
    In chants when the seasons swing

The moon in Sparta high   450
All through the night
Or in Athens rich and bright.
So, your death bequeaths
Such songs, and leaves
Lays for the music-makers.

1 : I wish it were in my power   [*Strophe 2*]   455
I wish I could ferry you back
Across the infernal water[8]
Beyond the crying river:
Rowed into the light.
For only you—so loving a wife—   460
Rescued your husband from Hades
In change for your life.
2 : Let the dust rest on you lightly, my Lady,
And let us despise him, your children and I,
If ever your husband elects a new wife.   465

3 : For the sake of the son she bore   [*Antistrophe 2*]
His mother would not inter
Her body beneath the earth.
Nor would his ancient sire:
Too selfish both by far
To redeem their son, though their hair   470
Was white as hoar.
2 : But you in your youth and bloom
Were willingly quenched for him
And relinquished the light.
1 : Could I be paired with so loving a wife
(A rare thing in life)
Long should I cleave to her   475
And live without strife.

Second Episode

[*hardly has* ALCESTIS' *body been carried into the house, followed by* ADMETUS *and the children, when* HERACLES,[9] *with
lion skin and club, approaches*]

HERACLES [*bluff, hail-fellow-well-met, hearty*]
Friends, dwellers in this land of Pherae,
do I happen on Admetus in his home?
LEADER. Yes, Heracles, Admetus is at home.
What brings you into Thessaly—
above all to this town of Pherae?   480
HERACLES. I have a labor[1] to perform for King Eurýstheus.

---

8. *The infernal water*: the River Styx.
9. *Heracles*: represented drunk, a stock
figure in Greek comedies of the period.
1. *A labor*: the eighth of the twelve fan-
tastic labors Heracles had to perform for
King Eurýstheus, his elder by two
months. This task had been decreed by
Zeus.

LEADER. On your way to where? On what errand?

HERACLES. To fetch the four-horse team of Diomédes, king of Thrace.

LEADER. And how will you manage that?
Have you no inkling with whom you deal?

HERACLES. Hardly. I've never put a foot in his domain. 485

LEADER. You'll not win those steeds without a fight.

HERACLES. No doubt, but then I never flinch before the job in hand.

LEADER. Kill then or be killed. Stay there dead or come back quick.

HERACLES. It's not the first time that I've run that risk.

LEADER. And when you've overthrown their keeper, what is next? 490

HERACLES. The horses. I shall drive them off to Tiryns.

LEADER. Having put the bit between their jaws? That won't be easy.

HERACLES. Why? Do they snort out fire?

LEADER. No, but with their teeth they tear men into tatters.

HERACLES. Flesh is for mountain beasts: not proper feed for horses. 495

LEADER. Wait till you see their mangers splashed with gore!

HERACLES. And their trainer—whose son does he proclaim himself?

LEADER. Son of Ares, and master of the Thracian shield of gold.

HERACLES. Phew! Another test of strength—just as you say:
hard going always, uphill work . . . 500
It looks as though I have to take on *all* the sons of Ares:[2]
First it was Lycáon, then Cycnus,
and now for the third duel I must grapple
with those horses and their master.
But no one shall ever live to see Alcmena's[3] son 505
cowering before some strong-armed bruiser.

LEADER. But look, the master of this realm himself comes out:
Admetus from his palace.

enter ADMETUS *with shaven head and dressed in black, followed by attendants similarly accoutred*]

ADMETUS. Welcome, son of Zeus and scion of Perseus.

HERACLES. And joy to you, Admetus, king of Thessaly. 510

ADMETUS. Ah, if that were only possible! But thank you all the same.

HERACLES. It seems you are in mourning. Why the shaven head?

ADMETUS. [*hedging*] I have to go and bury someone . . . someone dear.

HERACLES. Nothing's happened to any of your children? Heaven forbid!

ADMETUS. My children are alive and well inside the house. 515

HERACLES. Your father, then? . . . But he was ripe to go.

ADMETUS. He's quite himself, Heracles. And so is my mother.

HERACLES. It's not your wife, is it? Not Alcestis gone?

ADMETUS. Ah, there, I have a double tale to tell!

---

2. *Ares*: the god of war, called by the Latins Mars.
3. *Alcmena's son*: Heracles, whose mother was Alcmena and his father Zeus. Zeus came to Alcmena disguised as her husband, Amphitryon.

HERACLES. What do you mean? Is she alive or is she dead?   520
ADMETUS. She is and yet she isn't. It's most disturbing.
HERACLES. I'm none the wiser. You talk in riddles, man.
ADMETUS. She had a special rendezvous with Fate. Didn't you know?
HERACLES. I knew she'd pledged herself to die for you.
ADMETUS. So cannot . . . go on living . . . if she gave her word.   525
HERACLES. Well then, keep your tears for when it happens.
ADMETUS. The doomed are dead. The dead are not alive.
HERACLES. Naturally! To be or not be: there is a difference.
ADMETUS. You put it your way, Heracles; I'll put it mine.
HERACLES. Whom *are* you mourning, then? Some dead friend?   530
ADMETUS. A lady. A lady much . . . in our thoughts just now.
HERACLES. Some remote acquaintance or a relative?
ADMETUS. Remote in origin, but—very close to home.
HERACLES. How did she come to pass away inside your house?
ADMETUS. Her father was dead. She found a haven here.   535
HERACLES [*gathering his lion skin about him as if preparing to go*]
  Sad, sad! Admetus . . .
  Sorry I didn't find you less lugubrious.
ADMETUS. [*apprehensively*] What do you mean by that? What
  do you intend?
HERACLES. To propose myself as guest . . . in some other home.
ADMETUS. [*embarrassed*] My good sir, God forbid! That would
  be a disaster.
HERACLES. But visitors are a nuisance to a house in mourning.   540
ADMETUS. The dead are dead. Please step inside.
HERACLES. Make merry while friends mourn? It's unthinkable.
ADMETUS. No, you'd be in the guest wing—quite apart.
HERACLES. A thousand thanks but . . . just let me go.
ADMETUS. To put up with someone else? Out of the question.   545
  [*turns to a servant*]
  You there, escort this gentleman
  to the guest wing that adjoins the palace, and open it up.
    Tell those in charge to lay out lots of food,
  and shut the doors of the central court:
  to disturb a guest's enjoyment with the sounds of mourning
  is outrageous.   550
  [HERACLES *follows the servant out*]
LEADER. What are you doing, Admetus?
  In the midst of calamity,
  and you think of entertaining? . . . Are you mad?
ADMETUS. You mean, you'd think much more of me if I turned him
  out?
    Expelled a guest from house and town?
    Surely not! My being unfriendly
  does nothing to reduce my woes.   555
    It simply piles one evil on another
  and gets my house the name Unfriendly Hall.

What is more,
whenever *I* go to the thirsty land of Argos,
I find this same fellow the best of hosts.   560
LEADER. Why then do you try to hide the presence of death
if he comes here as your friend, as you say yourself?
ADMETUS. Because if he'd had an inkling of my present sorrows
he never would have stepped inside this house.
Some, I dare say, will think my action foolish   565
and give me less than credit for it,
but to be discourteous and turn a guest away
is unheard of underneath my roof.
          [*exit* ADMETUS *into the palace*]

SECOND CHORAL ODE

[*the* CHORUS *sings in praise of* ADMETUS' *hospitality, both
past and present, and of the wonderful sojourn of* APOLLO]
1. Guest-blessed house of the great
              everlastingly free:
      Graced with a visit no less   570
              than by lyric Apollo;
      In your halls he consented to be
      A herdsman, and piped in the hills
      And valleys love-ditties
              for shepherds to sheep.   575

2. The parded leopards in love   [*Antistrophe* 1]
              with his music agreed
      To mingle with sheep and feed.
              And the blood-flickered pride   580
      Of lions came leaping down
              from thickets and dens,
      And milk-speckled fawns
              tiptoeing from under the high   585
      Umbrella of pines
      Danced round the lyre of Apollo
              with neat little feet:
      Gay with the zest of his tunes.

3. Therefore does this monarch possess   [*Strophe* 2]
      Lands that are rich with cattle along
      The shores of the rippling lake Boebía.   590
      His arable fields stretch far away
      And his prairies spread to the somber stables
      Of the sun god's steeds
              in the deep Molossian range.
      The Aegean Sea is the term of his sway   595
              and the harborless shores of Mount Pelion.

1. And now again, though with eyelids wet   [*Antistrophe* 2]

He has opened his doors wide to his guest,
Yet laments in his house the loss of his late   600
Well-beloved spouse. For the gentleman born
Cannot err but in generous wise.
In the noble all wisdom resides,
Oh, it amazes!
And so in my soul the conviction abides
That the gentle and reverent man
        shall always fare well.   605

Third Episode

[*there is the sound of funeral music. A procession of
attendants led by* ADMETUS *and carrying the body of* ALCES-
TIS *on a bier issues from the palace. They are followed by
servants bearing offerings for the late departed*]

ADMETUS. Men of Pherae, your presence here is salutary and kind.
    You see my people carrying Alcestis' body
raised aloft, all decked for burial and the funeral pyre.
    Salute the dead, as custom is,
and speed her on her final way.   610
    [*the old man* PHERES, *with attendants carrying gifts, is seen
    approaching*]

LEADER. I see your father coming—with his old man's gait—
    his servants bearing presents for your wife:
adornments for the dead.
    [*enter* PHERES]

PHERES. I am come here, full of sympathy for you, my son.
    You have lost—and no one can deny it—
a noble wife, a virtuous wife.   615
    But such things must be borne, grievous though they be.
    [*he holds out an offering*]
Accept this present
and let it go with her into the grave.
    We must pay our homage to the corpse of her
who is dead instead of you, my son;   620
and saved me too from being without a child:
deprived of you, decrepit, in a sad and old decline.
    Her life, the sheer courage of her act,
is a shining light to womankind.
    [*stretches out his hand toward the bier*]
Savior of my son,   625
Who raised me up when I was down:
Fare you well.
May you be blessed in Hades' realm.
    [*turning back toward* ADMETUS]
This is the kind of marriage, to my mind,
that does the most for humankind . . .
otherwise why marry?

ADMETUS. [*pushing away the proffered offering*] Quite unasked by
   me, you come here to this burial
   and quite emphatically not my friend.   630
      Never shall she put your present on.
      Nothing of yours is she lacking for her tomb.
      There was a time for you to feel for me:
   when I was at the point of death.
      Then you stood aside and let another die:
   yes, the young die for the old,   635
   and now come whining over this dead body.
      Can you really be my father standing here?
      Can the one who said she bore me, called my mother,
   have really brought me forth?
      Or am I son of slave's blood.
   put to your woman's breast and sucking secretly?
      You showed your true self in the test.   640
      I count myself as not your son.
      Oh, you are a master coward!
      Senile, at the verge of life,
   yet lack the heart—oh, no, the guts—
   to lay your life down for your son . . .   645
   and have to let this woman do it—outsider to our blood.
      She is the one, and she alone,
   I have the right to look upon
   as both my mother and my father.
      And yet it would have been a lovely thing
   to win that battle for my life
   by dying for your child.
      How brief a fraction, after all,
   was left for you to live.   650
      You had enjoyed
   every happiness a man could ask:
   kingship in your prime, and me for son and heir   655
   to save you dying childless,
   your unprotected house a prey to strangers.
      Nor can you say it was because
   I disrespected your gray hairs
   that you deserted me to die.
      I always honored you. I made a point of it.
      and this is the thanks I earn   660
   from you and from my mother.
      Well, lose no time:
   get yourself an offspring to pamper your old age,
   and deck you out and wind your cerement when you are dead.
      For *I* shan't lift a hand to bury you.   665
      To you I am already dead;
   and if in fact I look upon the light
   it is because I found another savior.
      I am that person's child, I say,

devoted to that person till old age.
The dotards' prayers to die are insincere:
they grumble of old age and life's long span,   670
but once let death come near,
not one desires to go, and age becomes quite dear.

LEADER. Admetus, stop!
There is enough unhappiness
as things are.
Do not drive your father to a fury
and too far.

PHERES. My boy,
whom do you imagine you berate: 675
one of your bought Lydian or Phrygian slaves?
I am a Thessalian, don't you know:
a true son-and-free of a Thessalian sire.
You overreach yourself.
You fling your adolescent words at me to wound.   680
You shall not go unscathed.
I brought you into the world and brought you up,
to be master of this house.
Ought I now to die for you?
Is this the custom handed down—
that fathers die for sons? The Greek tradition?
It was never handed down to *me*.
You were born for your own good or ill.   685
Whatever is your due from me, you've had.
You enjoy wide power
and wide acres I shall leave to you,
just as my father left the same to *me*.
Do I harm you? How?
Do I rob you? Of what?
There's no more call for me to die for you   690
than you for me.

You enjoy the light of day.
Do you think your father doesn't?
Oh yes, he reckons life is sweet
just because it is so short
and eternity below so long.
You fought against your dying without a blush.
You live because you went beyond your span.   695
You killed this woman,
yet *I'm* the coward, you say.
O, poltroon—
shown up by the wife that died for you,
you brave, beautiful young man!
So smart you've found a way to live forever,
if a current wife will die instead.   700
But don't revile your friends

if they won't do the same.
So, be quiet, you degenerate, and remember
that if *you* love your life, so does everybody.
And if you speak ill of us,
listen to a mass of ill of you—and true.   705
LEADER. Ill—there's been too much already.
Please stop, old man, railing at your son.
ADMETUS. Speak on. I've said my say.
If he is hurt to hear the truth,
he shouldn't have hurt *me*.
PHERES. It would have been a greater hurt to die for you.   710
ADMETUS. So, there's no difference between a young and old man's
death?
PHERES. We are allotted one life each, not two.
ADMETUS. And you'd make yours as long as Zeus's, wouldn't you?
PHERES. Must you insult your own blameless father?
ADMETUS. Yes, because I see a glutton for long life.   715
PHERES. Aren't *you* the one that's substituting corpses at this
funeral?
ADMETUS. Precisely. Which just shows how pusillanimous you are.
PHERES. She did not die for me. That you cannot say.
ADMETUS. You just wait. One day you'll really come to need me.
PHERES. Meanwhile, keep up the wife supply: let more women die. 72‹
ADMETUS. To your disgrace: your cringing fear of death.
PHERES. The light of day is lovely: god-given light and lovely.
ADMETUS. Sir, your soul is small: has nothing manly in it.
PHERES. At least it's not old me you're carrying off with glee.[4]
ADMETUS. No, when that time comes what a paltry funeral it will be! 72‹
PHERES. It won't concern me, men's opinion, once I'm dead.
ADMETUS. Just listen to him. The senile have no self-respect what-
ever.
PHERES. Self-respect? Had *she*? Or was she just a simpleton to you?
ADMETUS. Will you kindly leave, and let me bury my dead.
PHERES. I am going. You murdered her and you can bury her.   730
You will answer to her kin for it.
If Acastus is even half a man
he will require something for his sister's life.
    [PHERES *gathers himself together and departs with his serv-
    ants.* ADMETUS *shouts after him.*]
ADMETUS. Go, you, and that woman too who lives with you.
Grow old together: a barren pair, as you deserve.   735
Never come beneath my roof again.
If I had to make a proclamation,
blazing forth my break with you and yours—
I'd make that proclamation now.
    [*he turns back to the bier*]
Let us move ɔn, bear our burden as we may,
and lay this body on its pyre.   740

4. Euripides rhymes three lines here, this one and the ones before and after.

[*exeunt* ADMETUS *and cortege while the* CHORUS *chants a short dirge for* ALCESTIS]

CHORUS. Poor brave and blighted lady
 Great and best of ladies, go.
 Goodbye to you. May gentle Hermes[5]
 Pilot you: received by Hades.
 And if down there the good have merit,   745
 Sit beside the bride of Pluto.[6]

  [*enter* BUTLER, *disgusted*]

BUTLER. Every sort of visitor, from every sort of land,
 I've known and waited on in Admetus' house,
 but this visitor today   750
 is the worst I've ever had to entertain.
 First, though he sees our master is in mourning,
 he strides right in and makes himself at home without a blush.
 Then, with no consideration for our feelings,
 he isn't satisfied with what we have to offer
 but hollers out for what we haven't brought.   755
 He grabs the loving-cup with ivy round it
 and swills it down like so much grape juice.
 Of course, the wine's black fire wraps him around:
 he's in a blaze.
 He puts twigs of myrtle on his head
 and bellows unmelodiously.   760
 There is a double discord going on:
 his unstanchable cacophanies
 (which utterly ignore Admetus' loss)
 and our household lamentations for our mistress.
 Even so, in accordance with our master's wish,
 we show dry eyes to him, this visitor
 —this robber bandit, probably—
 whom here I am regaling in this house,   765
 when from that house my Lady's gone . . .
 and I did not even follow her last walk
 or lift my hand to say farewell.
 and she was like a mother to me—
 and all us servants.
 She fended off a thousand ills   770
 and calmed her husband down.
 Am I not right to loathe
 this insensitive, intruding man?

  [HERACLES *lurches in, garlanded, cup in hand*]

HERACLES. You there, why that glum and priggish look?
 A servant shouldn't wear a vinegary face
 —not for a guest—he ought to beam and serve.   775
 You see your master's friend approach, and scowl

---

5. *Hermes*: the messenger of the gods (Latin name: *Mercury*).
6. *The bride of Pluto*: Persephone, the queen of the underworld. (The Greeks called Pluto *Hades*, and the Latins called Persephone *Proserpine*.)

with a face like doom,
sunk in some private worry of your own.
  Come over here and learn a thing or two.
  Do you understand the secret of mortality?   780
  I don't suppose you do. How should you?
  Listen to me.
  Take death:
all men have to pay that debt
yet not one man jack of them can tell
if he'll be around tomorrow.
  Fortune is mysterious. The march of events.   785
  It can't be taught or caught by any trick.
  There:
I've told you now and now you know—and now cheer up.
  Have a drink and think:
each day is yours to live—just as it comes—
the rest is luck.
  And one more thing:
pay homage to the sweetest power of all   790
—Aphrodite—
mankind's most gracious goddess.
  For the rest, forget it . . .
but don't forget my words.
  They do make sense, eh? Do they not?
  I think they do.
   [*he lifts his cup*]
  Therefore let your heartache go—it's overdone.
  Quaff with me and rise above it.   795
  I have no doubt the wine
splashing in your cup will change your mood
and free you from your present dumps.
  We are but human. We should keep a human mind.
  You solemn scowling worriers,   800
every one of you—so far as I can tell—
do *not* lead lives but plain catastrophes.
BUTLER. We know all this, but our position here
  hardly calls for fun and games.
HERACLES. The dead woman's an outsider, eh?   805
  Why overdo the grief?
After all, your lord and lady are alive.
BUTLER. Alive? So you know nothing of our sorrows here?
HERACLES. Well, no . . . unless your master lied to me.
BUTLER. He's just too kind, too hospitable.
HERACLES. Hospitable? Neglecting me for some outsider dead? 810
BUTLER. Outsider? Oh, she *is* an outsider now, all right.
HERACLES. Ha! There's something that he didn't tell me, eh?
BUTLER. Please . . . go in peace. Our master's woes are our concern.
  [*he turns to go, but* HERACLES *seizes him*]
HERACLES. So it wasn't really all about some dead outsider?
BUTLER. No. That's what so upset me when I saw you rollicking. 815

HERACLES. But that's terrible: my host has tricked me.
BUTLER. You came here at a time not suitable for guests.
  We are in mourning: you see our shaven heads, our funeral
  black.
HERACLES. Who is dead then? One of the children? Surely not!   820
  ... His old father?
BUTLER. [*hesitating*] If you must, sir: it's Admetus' wife ... Yes,
  she's gone forever.
HERACLES. [*slowly putting down his cup*] What are you saying?
  ... And he went and welcomed me!
BUTLER. He was ashamed to turn you from his house.
HERACLES. Poor man—what a soulmate he has lost!
BUTLER. We are all lost, not she alone.   825
HERACLES. Yes, I felt it. I saw it in his eyes—the brimming—
  in his shaven head, his face.
    But when he said it was a stranger's funeral,
  I was convinced
  and against my deeper instinct passed in through these doors,
  made merry in this kind man's house   830
  while he was in this state ...
    [*he begins to tear off his wreaths*]
  What—garlanded and in my cups
  and you didn't say a thing! ... The whole house laid flat!
  Where is he burying her?
  Where can I go and find her?
BUTLER. Straight along the road that takes you to Larissa.   835
  You'll see a monument outside the village.
    [*exit* BUTLER]
HERACLES. Come, reckless heart and hand of mine,
  now show what sort of son Alcmena bore
  To Zeus—she queen of Tiryns—Electryon's child.
    I must go at once and save this lately dead: 840
  restore Alcestis to this home of hers,
  and make Admetus some return.
    [*begins to fasten his lion's skin securely*]
  I'll go and watch for Death—that gloom-draped king of
  corpses—
  —and I think I'll find him knocking back libations near the
  tomb.
  I'll leap out from ambush, grab him,   845
  weld my arms around him,
  and no matter how he heaves and strains
  no man alive shall prize him from my grip ...
  not until he's given back this woman.
    But if my quarry balks me,   850
  doesn't come to get his blood and porridge,[7]

7. *Porridge*: Euripides uses the word πελανος, which means a kind of gruel—the mixture of meal, honey, and oil offered to the gods. I take it he refers to this bait rather than to Alcestis. *Cora* or *Kora*: another name for Persephone, queen of the underworld.

I'll take myself below:
to mistress Cora and her husband's
sun-starved establishment, and do my asking there.
    I am quite certain
I shall fetch Alcestis up and place her in the arms
of my most generous host,
who made me at home and did not turn me out   855
though he was struck to the heart with grief;
yes, who hid his feelings, heroic man, and did me honor.
    Is there anyone in Thessaly more hospitable than he?
    Anyone in Greece?
    Never let him say that such nobility
was answered by a lack of generosity.   860

[HERACLES *hurries out just as the funeral procession is heard returning.* ADMETUS *enters with his train*]

Fourth Episode

ADMETUS. Oh, my return to my home is return to lament
    Oh, the emptiness left in unwelcoming rooms!
    Go where? Be where? What say? What not?
    I wish I were dead.
    What doom-laden womb, what mother produced me?   865
    I yearn for the shades. I lust after phantoms.
    Theirs are the homes I crave to indwell.
    The joy in my eyes is a light gone dim.
    The joy in the tread of my feet is gone.
    Death has cleft from me half my life: 870
    Traded to Hades.

CHORAL DIALOGUE

CHORUS. Enter, enter into your home's retreat.   [*Strophe* 1]
ADMETUS. Aiai!
CHORUS. You've suffered enough to make you cry.
ADMETUS. Weep. Aiai!
CHORUS. I understand. I know the ordeal.
ADMETUS. Heave. Aiai!
CHORUS. It is no help to her below.   875
ADMETUS. Grieve. Aiai!
CHORUS. To miss forever the face of your beloved
    Is bitter indeed.
ADMETUS. The mere recall of it batters my heart.
    What greater pain can any man face
    Than suffer the loss of a faithful wife?
    I wish I had never married or lived   880
    Inside this house with her I loved.
    I covet the ones who never wed:
    The childless ones—their single life
    Only a measured grief begets.

The ills of children, the nuptial bed   885
Scattered by death, are all regrets
Compared to lives that can be led
Single and with no child instead.

CHORUS. Fate, fate, ineluctable fate!   [*Antistrophe* 1]
ADMETUS. Aiai!
CHORUS. Your lamentation has no limit.
ADMETUS. Cry. Aiai!   890
CHORUS. It is a bitter load to bear, but . . .
ADMETUS. Heave. Aiai!
CHORUS. Bear up, you're not the first to lose . . .
ADMETUS. Grieve. Aiai!
CHORUS. A wife. Disaster strikes in many a guise
    At other mortals and in other ways.
ADMETUS. The long sorrow, love's lost lament   895
    For those under the ground . . .
    Why did you hold me back from the leap
    Into the grave that gaped,
    There to lie dead with her
    Who has no human peer?
    Hades would then have been able to take   900
    Two devoted souls, not one,
    To cross the land of the nether lake.

CHORUS. There was in my own   [*Strophe* 2]
    Family a man whose only son
    Died in his home: 905
    A youth well worth his tears.
    Yet *he* measured his grief, this childless man,
    Although his locks had turned
    White and he had gone
    Far into life.   910
ADMETUS. [*unable to proceed into the house*] This palace, my
    home, how shall I go in?
    How shall I dwell with luck's reverse:
    Everything changed, everything worse?
    Once by torchlight, wedding songs ringing,   915
    Holding her hand, I went in.
    And after us came the revelers singing,
    Cheering my dead one, cheering me.
    A beautiful couple, that we were
    And seen to be
    Noble and rich.   920
    But now instead of the wedding march
    and glittering clothes, you send me in
    Vested in dark
    To a lonely, dismal, empty couch.   925

CHORUS. To shatter your bliss   [*Antistrophe* 2]

This unrehearsable sorrow struck.
Nevertheless
It saved your life and soul.
Your consort has gone, deserted her love.   930
Is this so strange? Many a man
Death has divided from his spouse.

ADMETUS. Friends, my wife's fate is happier than mine,   935
I think, although it might not seem to be:
for now no pain shall ever touch her—
a thousand worries she has stopped with glory.
But I, who have not title to be living,
have overstepped my mark and must drag out
a bitter life . . . I realize it now.   940
How shall I bear to go into my empty home?
Whom shall I greet inside? By whom be welcomed?
Which way to look?
The wilderness in there shall drive me out:
the empty bed, her favorite seats, their very sight;   945
the floors unswept throughout the house;
then the children clinging to my lap and crying
for their mother.
And the servants all in tears
for that tender queen this house has lost.
Thus will it be at home,   950
but in the world outside . . . ah!
Young unmarried women with weddings in their eyes
will frighten me away—
buzzing around in female swarms . . .
No, I shall not be able to brave the sight
of my wife's compeers.
And those who have no time for me
will sieze their chance and say:
"Look, the cheap coward   955
alive and well, who ran away from death:
so small he got his wife to die instead . . .
Is he a man, do you think? He execrates his parents
but could not die himself."
Yes, that's the charming reputation I shall earn,
on top of all my sorrows.
Tell me, dear friends,
is there any point in going on—   960
with such a reputation, such a record?

THIRD CHORAL ODE

[the CHORUS *sings of implacable Necessity and the impossi-
bility of raising the dead. And yet* ALCESTIS' *choice was
beautiful*]

High as the Muses I   [*Strophe* 1]
Have sung and searched the sky

Where great ideas lie
But never have found as yet
A greater thing than fate.   965
Nor any drug in Thrace
Listed or engraved
By Orpheus; not his voice,
Nor what Apollo gave
Asclepius and his race.   970
No anodyne that can
Cure the fate of man.

Necessity alone   [*Antistrophe 1*]
Although she is divine
Is approached by none
Through effigy or shrine.
She heeds no sacrifice.   975
O Mistress, do not move
To make me less alive,
For even mighty Zeus
Needs you to fulfill
His work and so his will.
Chalybian steel   980
Is far less hard, for she'll
Bend to none or feel
Soft for us.

And now in the vice of her grip,   [*Strophe 2*]   985
Admetus, she has you fast.
   Bear it, for never will weeping
   Raise the gone from the dead.
   Even the children of gods
   Death fades into his shades.   990
   Loved she was among us
   Loved will she be though dead.
   The noblest woman you could
   Harness to your bed.

Never think of her tomb as the same [*Antistrophe 2*]   995
As the mounds of the dead gone by
But more like a shrine of the gods
And a pilgrim's place to pray.
Climbing the path that winds   1000
A passerby will say:
"Here lies she who saved
Her consort. Now is she
A hallowed spirit. I
Salute you, Lady, bless us."
Thus will pilgrims cry.   1005
LEADER. Ah! here comes Alcmena's son, Admetus.
   It looks as though he's making for your home.
      [*enter* HERACLES, *leading a woman heavily veiled*]

Exodus or Denouement

HERACLES. One should be candid with a friend, Admetus:
　　not keep grudges buried deep inside.
　　Coming upon you in your hour of sorrow　　　　　　1010
　I might have thought to share it like a friend.
　　Why then did you never tell me
　the body that you had to bury was your wife's?
　　You made me at home and welcomed me
　as if the one you mourned were just a far-off friend.
　　I went and wreathed my head quite merrily　　　　1015
　and tossed libations to the gods—
　all in a stricken house.
　　　　[*wagging his finger*]
　　That was reprehensible of you . . . reprehensible . . .
　but I shall not tax you with it
　seeing how great your present sufferings are.
　　Well, what I've come back to tell you is:
　take this woman and keep her for me please,　　　　1020
　till I return here with the Thracian steeds,
　having done Diomédes in—the Bistonians' king.
　　If I fail to come back safe and sound,
　she is yours to fetch and carry in your home.
　　She came into my hands through much hard work.　1025
　　It was a local public contest
　organized by people that I met:
　a real test of strength for athletes.
　　That's her origin. I took her as a prize.
The winners in the lighter heats led horses off,　　　　1030
　but in the major events—boxing and wrestling—
　the prize was cattle. A woman was thrown in.
　　To decline such a splendid offering, once I'd won it,
　seemed to me a shame.
　　So, as I was saying,
　I put this woman in your care.
　　She isn't something I just grabbed:　　　　　　　　1035
　I won her with my sweat and blood.
　　In time, perhaps, you too will come to thank me.
ADMETUS. It was not to snub you, Heracles,
　or antagonize you in the least,
　that I hid my poor wife's fate from you,
　but had you taken off and gone to stay with someone else.　1040
it would have only added one anguish to another.
　　There were tears enough for the hurt I *had*.
　　As to this woman, I beg you, sir,
　if it is remotely possible,
　ask some other Thessalian—
　one who hasn't had to face what I have—
　to take care of her

You have many friends in Pherae.
Don't bring home my grief to me: 1045
I could not view her in the house and keep from tears.
  I am sick to the heart, weighted down with sorrow,
do not make me sicker.
  Where, moreover, in my house
could a young woman properly be lodged . . .
for young she seems to be, from her pretty style and dress.   1050
  Will the men's wing suit her for a home—
and she remain untouched lodging with young men?
For it is not easy, Heracles, to check a young man in his prime.
  I am only thinking of you.
  Or am I to intrude her into my dead wife's room,   1055
lodge her there?
  But how could I? . . . Give her my own wife's bed?
  I recoil from the double blame that might bring:
the charge first from some citizen
that I was being unfaithful to the one who saved me,
falling into bed with another woman, and a young one too;
then from the deceased herself—   1060
who so merits my adoration . . .
  Oh, I must be circumspect!
    [*he turns toward the veiled figure with a start . . . and a
    deep sigh*]
Young lady, whoever you are,
know you have the build and figure of Alcestis.
    [*he breaks away*]
By the gods! take the woman from my sight.   1065
Don't trample on a man that's down.
  For when I look at her, I'm looking at my wife, it seems:
my soul is in a turmoil; tears prick into my eyes.
  Stricken to the heart, at last I taste
the full peculiar bitterness of my fate.
LEADER. There's nothing good about your lot that I can say.   1070
  Heaven's visitations we must shoulder as we may.
HERACLES. I wish I had the power
to march your consort from the mansions underground
back into the light, and do a kindness to you.
ADMETUS. I'm well aware you would. There is no way, however.   1075
  The dead once dead never come to light.
HERACLES. Do not overshoot the mark. Take things quietly.
ADMETUS. And *that* is easier said than done.
HERACLES. What good is there in endless grief?
ADMETUS. None, I know. It is a love compels me.   1080
HERACLES. Yes, love for the dead compels our tears.
ADMETUS. Oh, she has ruined me more than I can utter!
HERACLES. You've lost a perfect wife: there's no denying.
ADMETUS. So perfect, I'll not enjoy this life again.
HERACLES. Time softens things. Now your grief is young.   1085

ADMETUS. Time, you say. If only time spelt death!

HERACLES. A new bride could change all that: the love of a woman.

ADMETUS. Be quiet. You don't know what you say. It's unthinkable.

HERACLES. What, never remarry? Hug an empty bed?

ADMETUS. No woman alive shall ever bed with me.   1090

HERACLES. And you imagine this will profit your departed wife?

ADMETUS. I must revere her wherever she may be.

HERACLES. Fine, fine, but just a little simple, don't you think?

ADMETUS. Very well, but do not make a bridegroom out of me.

HERACLES. I admire this unswerving dedication to your wife.   1095

ADMETUS. Even though she's gone, I'd rather die than be unfaithful.

HERACLES. Then receive this woman into your stately home.

ADMETUS. No, I beg you, by Zeus who is your father.

HERACLES. You'll be making a mistake if you refuse.

ADMETUS. And I'll be wounded to the heart if I accept.   1100

HERACLES. Have faith. This little favor may turn out to be your gain.

ADMETUS. I wish to God you'd never won that competition.

HERACLES. And yet, you are going to share in what I won.

ADMETUS. Nice of you to say so, but the woman has to go.

HERACLES. If she must, she must. But let's consider *if* she must. 1105

ADMETUS. She must. Unless of course it makes you hate me.

HERACLES. I insist, and I know exactly what I'm doing.

ADMETUS. All right, you win. But it doesn't give me pleasure.

HERACLES. One day you'll thank me. Just trust me now.

ADMETUS. [*turning to the servants*] Take her in then . . . since I *have* to have her in my house.   1110

HERACLES. I'm not placing her in any servant's hands.

ADMETUS. Then take her in yourself, if that's what you would rather.

HERACLES. I'd rather place her in *your* hands.

ADMETUS. And I'd rather keep her off them . . . Can't she just walk in?

HERACLES. Only in the security of your own right hand.   1115

ADMETUS. Sir, you are forcing me against my will.

HERACLES. Just take the risk. Put out a hand and touch her.

ADMETUS. [*gingerly, with the tips of his fingers, and looking away*] My hand is out.

HERACLES. You look as though you were beheading a Medusa.
Have you got her?

ADMETUS. I have.

HERACLES. Then hold on to her.
And one day you'll say that Zeus's son
was a most rewarding guest to entertain.   1120
  [*steps toward the figure and lifts her veil*]
Take a look at her.
Does she strike you like . . . your wife?
  [*as* ADMETUS *staggers back*]

Let your tears give place to joy.

ADMETUS. O you gods, what shall I say? A wishful apparition?
Am I really looking at my wife?
Or is this ecstasy some heavenly delusion?   1125

HERACLES. No delusion, truly. You really see your wife.

ADMETUS. Are you sure she's not a ghost from the other side?

HERACLES. That would make your guest a spirit-raiser.

ADMETUS. But is she—do I see—the wife I buried?

HERACLES. Certainly you do. I don't wonder you mistrust your luck. 1130

ADMETUS. My wife! I touch her. Is she real? Can I address her?

HERACLES. Address her by all means. You have your heart's desire.

ADMETUS. Sweet wife! Sweet face! Sweet form!
Beyond all hope I hold you—
whom I never thought to see again.

HERACLES. You hold her, yes: and may no deity be jealous.   1135

ADMETUS. Most illustrious son of mighty Zeus,
be blessed forever. Your father keep you.
You alone have raised me up . . .
But how ever did you bring her back from dark to light?

HERACLES. By battling with the Lord of Ghosts.

ADMETUS. Battling with Death, you mean? Where was that?   1140

HERACLES. Beside the tomb. I darted out and locked him in my grip.

ADMETUS. [*troubled*] My lady stands. She makes no comment. Why?

HERACLES. It is forbidden that she talk with you   1145
until three days have passed and she is purged
of her consecration to the powers below.
But you—escort her in . . . And, Admetus, for the future,
continue as you are: a friend to wanderers.
So, farewell.
I must go and wrestle with the labor set for me
by that king, the son of Sthenelus.[8]   1150

ADMETUS. No, stay, and make your home with us.

HERACLES. Another time . . . I must be getting on.

ADMETUS. The best of luck, then. Come this way again.

[*exit* HERACLES. ADMETUS *turns to the citizens of Pherae*]

ADMETUS. To every township and province in my realm
I proclaim a festival of choruses and dance   1155
to celebrate these great events.
Let altars fume with sacrifice of kine.
We have our former state transformed
to a better kind of life.
I shall not disavow that I am happy now.
[ADMETUS *leads* ALCESTIS *into the palace*]

CHORUS. Many the forms of divine intervention
Many the marvels the gods entertain.
What was expected was never accomplished.   1160
What was impossible God found a way to.
So ended this story today.

8. *The son of Sthenelus*: Eurýstheus.

Medea

Characters

NURSE
TUTOR *to Medea's sons*
MEDEA, *Asiatic princess*
CHORUS *of Corinthian women*
CREON, *king of Corinth*
JASON, *husband of Medea*
AEGEUS, *king of Athens*
MESSENGER
TWO BOYS, *sons of Medea*
HANDMAIDS *of Medea*
ATTENDANTS AND GUARDS *for Creon and Aegeus*

Time and Setting

It is midmorning outside Jason's house in Corinth. Ten years have passed since the Argonauts sailed home after finding the Golden Fleece. During that time, Jason and Medea [the Asian bride he brought back with him] have been living modestly in Corinth: models of an unassailable married life of devotion to each other and their children. But the news has just broken that Jason is to marry the daughter of the king of Corinth. [The exit on stage left leads to the town and royal palace, that on the right to the country].

> [enter the NURSE from the house. She is an old woman who has looked after MEDEA from babyhood. Her face, the only part of her showing from the dark, heavy clothes that envelop her, is puckered with age and distress]

Prologue

NURSE. Why did the winged oars of the Argo[1]
ever weave between those gnashing blue
fjords towards the land of Colchis?
    Why did the pines in the dells of Pelion[2]
ever fall to the axe and fill
the rowing hands of heroes sent by Pelias[3]   5
to fetch the Golden Fleece?
    My mistress, Medea, then
never would have sailed to Iolcus with its towers

---

1. *Argo*: the ship in which Jason and his companions sailed on the quest for the Golden Fleece.
2. *Pelion*: a mountain in northern Greece.

3. *Pelias*: When Jason came to claim the kingdom of Iolcus, from which Pelias had expelled Jason's father, Pelias sent him to get the Golden Fleece.

or been struck to the heart with love of Jason.
   She never would have baited Pelias' daughters
to the murder of their father[4]   10
and be living here in Corinth[5] now
with her husband and her children . . .
   Ah, she has merited this city's good opinion,
exile though she came,
and was in everything Jason's perfect foil,
being in marriage that saving thing:
a wife who does not go against her man.   15
     [*with a despairing glance toward the house*]
   Now everything has turned to hate,
her passion to a plague.
   Jason has betrayed his sons and her,
takes to bed a royal bride,
Creon's daughter—the king of Corinth's.
   Medea, spurned and desolate,   20
breaks out in oaths,
invokes the solemnest vows,
calls the gods to witness
how Jason has rewarded her.
   She does not eat,
lies prostrate, slumped in anguish,
wastes away in day-long tears.   25
   Ever since she heard of Jason's perfidy
she has not raised her eyes
or looked up from the floor.
   She might be a rock or wave of the sea,
for all she heeds of sympathy from friends,
except sometimes to tilt her pale head away   30
and moan to herself about her father—
whom she loved—
and her country and the home she sacrificed[6]
to journey here
with a man—oh—who so disdains her now.
   Yes, now she knows
at a terrible first hand
what it is to miss one's native land.   35
     [*she pauses; almost whispers the next words*]
   She hates her sons.
   Takes no pleasure in their sight.
   I dread to think
of what is hatching in her mind.

---

4. *She never . . . murder of their father*:
Medea, a sorceress by reputation, tricked
Pelias' daughters into cutting their father into pieces and boiling them, on the
pretext that this would magically restore
him to youth. Her revenge on Pelias, who
had murdered Jason's father Aeson during Jason's absence on the quest for the
Golden Fleece, was successful.

5. Jason and Medea were expelled from
the kingdom, and they took refuge in
Corinth, a wealthy city and rival of
Athens, located on the isthmus between
the Péloponnese and Attica.
6. *Home she sacrificed:* Medea had
helped Jason take the Golden Fleece
away from her own father's kingdom.

She is a fierce spirit:
takes no insult lying down.
I know her well. She frightens me:⁷ 39
a dangerous woman, and
anyone who crosses her
will not easily sing a song of triumph. 45
But here come the boys after their run:
suspecting nothing of a mother's tragedy . . .
Oh, it is true—
unhappy thoughts and youth never go together.

[*enter* TUTOR *with* TWO BOYS, *aged about eight and ten.*
TUTOR *is an old man, dressed loosely in an ocher-colored
cloak. The boys are squeezed into shorts and have close-fit-
ting woolen caps on their heads. They hang about in the
background, laughing and talking, while the old man
advances*]

TUTOR. [*with a half-teasing familiarity*] Ah, Nurse!
Faithful old appendage of my Lady's home,
what are you doing here all forlorn,
standing moaning to yourself outside the gates? 50
Does Medea really want to be left alone?
NURSE. Ah, dogged old pedagogue of Jason's sons,
when a master's fortunes are struck down
the heart of a faithful slave is stricken too. 55
I am plunged in such a depth of grief
I came out here to tell the earth and sky
Medea's catastrophe.
TUTOR. What! Has the poor woman not stopped her crying yet?
NURSE. Stopped! You amaze me.
Her ordeal, far from halfway done, 60
hardly has begun.
TUTOR. Poor innocent fool—to be quite frank about our
mistress—
she knows little of the latest blow.
NURSE. Latest? What's that, old man?
Don't keep it from me.
TUTOR. Nothing, nothing . . . I'm sorry I even spoke.
NURSE. Come now, we're both slaves here, are we not?
By your own gray beard, do not hold it back . . . 65
I can keep a secret if I must.
TUTOR. Well, I'd gone to where the old dice-players sit,
near Pirene's sacred fountain,
and there I overheard (pretending not to listen)
someone say:
"Creon, this country's king,
is making plans to drive these boys from Corinth— 70

7. Lines 40–43 are bracketed by many
editors as doubtful. Dramatically they
are certainly a mistake:
*I am frightened she will slip
into the palace unawares,*
and in the nuptial bedroom
ram a sharp knife into Jason's side,
or even kill the King as well as
*   bridegroom*
and get herself a far worse doom.

their mother too"—
I don't know if the story's true.
I hope that it is not.
NURSE. No, surely no?
Jason would not let his sons be treated so,
however far he's parted from their mother.   75
TUTOR. [*grimly*] Old loves are left behind by new.
That man is not this house's friend.
NURSE. We're all finished, then—
if we ship this second wave
before we've bailed the first.
TUTOR. Now listen—
this is not the time to let our mistress know.   80
Just keep quiet about it—not a word.
NURSE. [*with an anguished glance over her shoulder, in a whisper*] Poor little boys,
do you hear how much your father's worth to you?
I wish he were . . .
   [*checks herself*]
no, not dead, he is my master still . . .
but, oh, what an enemy he's proved
to those he should have loved!
TUTOR. What human being is not?   85
Is this news to you,
that every person's dearest neighbor is himself:
some rightly so, some out of greed and selfishness.
This father does not love his sons, but—
his new wedding bed.
NURSE. Come along, boys, into the house.
Everything is going to be all right.
   [*dropping her voice*]
Keep them away as much as you can.   90
Do not let them near their mother.
so long as she is in this deadly mood.
Already I have caught her eyes on them:
the eyes of a mad bull.
There's something she is plotting
and her fury won't lie down—this I know—
until the lightning strikes and someone's felled.
Let us hope it's enemies, not friends.   95
   [*a long-drawn-out sob*—MEDEA's—*is heard from the house*] [8]
MEDEA. I am so unhappy—oh!
the misery of it! I wish I were dead.
NURSE. [*hustling the children toward the door*]
Listen—there . . . poor children, your mother,
Raking her heart up, raking her rage.
Quick, inside: into the house.   100

8. The next 116 lines in the Greek are cast in a different meter, which I trans- posed into the nearest English equiva- lent.

Don't come anywhere near her sight.
Don't approach. Beware, watch out
For her savage mood, destructive spleen:
Yes and her implacable will.
Off with you now; hurry inside.   105
Soon, I know, her fury will flare
Out from the slowly gathering cloud
What will she perpetrate then, I fear—
Proud, importunate willful soul—
   So bitterly spurned.   110
   [*exeunt* TUTOR *and* BOYS]
   [*a long-suppressed shout is heard from inside*: MEDEA'S
   voice]
MEDEA. Oh, what misery! Oh, what pain!
Cursed sons, and a mother for cursing!
Death take you all—you and your father:
   The whole house wither.
NURSE. [*sobbing*] Oh, how it grieves me!   115
Why make the sons
     share in their father's
Guilt? Oh, why
    should *they* be hated?
Poor young children, your danger appals me.
Ruthless is the temper of royalty:
Often commanding, seldom commanded;   120
Terribly slow to forgive and forget.
How much better to live among equals.
I want no part of greatness and glory:
Let me decline in a safe old age.
The very name of the "middle way"   125
Has health in it: is best for man.
Good never comes from overreaching,
And when it provokes the gods, it destroys   130
   All the more thoroughly.

PARODOS OR ENTRY SONG

   [*the* CHORUS *of Corinthian women enters, full of apprehen-
   sion and concern for* MEDEA]
CHORUS. I heard her voice, I heard her shout,
   It was the most unhappy
Woman from Colchis—far from calm yet—
   But tell me, old Nurse.
From the porch of the house, it moaned outside.   135
   O women, I cannot delight
In the pain of Jason's house:
A house I have loved very well.
NURSE. House there is none: life of it gone.
The master is had . . . by a princess's bed.   140

The mistress in her boudoir pines.
There are no words her friends can find
To touch her disconsolate heart.
MEDEA. [*in another spasm*] Ahhh!
Cleave my brain with a flash from the sky.
What good is left for me in living?   145
Alas! Alas! Come Death, unloose
My life from a life I loathe.

CHORUS. Listen, O Zeus and Earth and Light   [*Strophe*]
To the stricken tune of this plangent[9] wife.   150
And you, loveless lady,
What yearning for love on a bed of delight
Could make you hurry to death, the night?
Pray not for that.
If your husband has gone to adore   155
A new bride in his bed, why, this
Has often happened before.
Do not harrow your soul. For Zeus
Will succor your cause. What use
To lessen your life with grief
For a lost lord?
MEDEA. [*from inside*] O mighty Themis, and Artemis, Queen,[1] 160
For all the fine vows I bound him with,
See what my hated husband has done.
Grant me to watch him, at last, with his bride,
Palace and all, crumble in ruin.
How dare they do to me what they have done!   165
O Father, my country, the land I abandoned,
Flagrantly killing my brother.[2]
NURSE. Hear what she says
with her cry from the heart
To Themis and Zeus:
(goddess of rights
And he whom mankind
makes keeper of vows.)   170
Certainly soon
in no small way
Her fury will play itself out.

CHORUS. If she would come out and, face to face,   [*Antistrophe*]
Listen to what we have to say,   175
She might let go
This rampant anger, spite of soul.
I hope I never fail my friends.
So go, Nurse, entice her to come: 180

9. *Plangent*: lamenting.
1. *Themis*: justice. *Artemis*: guardian of women. Called Diana by the Latins.
2. *Killing my brother*: Medea slew her brother Absyrtus when she escaped with Jason, and tossed him piecemeal over the side of the ship, knowing that their pursuers would stop to pick the pieces up.

Say we are *with* her: we are her friends.
Hurry, before she does any harm
    To those inside . . .
Grief can swell to enormity.
NURSE. [*walking to the door*] I'll do my best, but am afraid   185
May *not* be able to persuade
        My Lady; and yet
    I am glad to shoulder the burden;
Although she glares with a bull-mad gaze
(Or is it a lioness with her whelps)
When anyone comes or speaks or helps.
        [*she turns at the door*]
    Oh, botchers and blunderers! Yes,   190
That's what they were, those artists of old:
Makers of music for life and joy,
For grand celebrations and groaning boards;
But, oh, nothing for sorrow and pain: 195
No music or song on hand-plucked lyre
    For the thing that brings death
And terrible endings to many a home.

    Oh, what a blessing is missed
        by having no music for this!   200
    What a waste of it, then
        by singing in vain,
    When fullness at feasts
        is its own joy and gain.
        [*exit* NURSE *into the house*]
CHORUS. Deep is her sobbing from depths of pain:
Shrill the news her suffering brings   205
Of marriage betrayed, a love gone wrong.
    Outraged, she
            importunate prays
    To Themis, the daughter of Zeus:
Keeper of vows, who sailed her through
    Those dangerous straits and the night
To Hellas[3] across the salt of the sea.   210

First Episode

[MEDEA *enters from the house, colorfully, even opulently,
dressed. She is wan and her eyes red with weeping, but she is
surprisingly calm and in control*]
MEDEA. Women of Corinth, be indulgent, please: 215
I have obeyed you and come out.
    The charge of aloofness—as I know too well—
is something often leveled
at both the retiring and the busy man.

3. *Hellas*: Greece.

He who chooses a quiet life
has this alleged against him too:
laziness and lack of spirit.
    Yes, public opinion has most shallow eyes.   220
    People hate at sight
a harmless human being,
knowing nothing of the real man.
    I agree, of course,
that a foreigner should conform,
adapt to his society . . .
and a citizen is censurable no less
when too self-centered or uncouth
to avoid offending his companions.
    Nevertheless, I . . .
       [*she breaks off with a pang*]
I . . . out of a clear sky
have been struck a blow that breaks my heart.   225
  My friends, it is over.
I want to die.
Life has lost all point.
The man who was my life
—and he knows it too—
has become for me beneath contempt.
       [*she surveys the women*]
    Of all the creatures that can feel and think,   230
we women are the worst-treated things alive.
    To begin with,
we bid the highest price in dowries
just to buy some man
to be dictator of our bodies . . .
    How that compounds the wrong!
    Then there is the terrifying risk: 235
Shall we get a good man or a bad?
    Divorce is a disgrace
(at least for women),
to repudiate the man, not possible.
    So, plunged into habits new to her,
conventions she has never known at home,
she has to guess like some clairvoyant
how to handle the man who shares her bed.   240
    And if we learn our lesson well
in this exacting role,
and our husband does not kick against the marriage yoke,
oh, ours is an enviable life!
    Otherwise, we are better dead.
    When a man gets bored with wife and home,
he simply roams abroad,   245
relieves the tedium of his spirit:
turns to a friend or finds his cronies.

We women, on the other hand,
turn only to a single man.
We live safe at home, they say.
They do battle with the spear.
How superficial!   250
I had rather stand my ground three times among the shields
than face a childbirth once.
Anyway,
your case and mine are not the same.
You have your city.
You have your father's home.
Life offers you the sweet fellowship of friends.
I am alone,   255
without a city, wronged by a husband,
uprooted from a foreign land.
I have no mother, brother, cousin;
am without a haven from this storm.
So, please, I ask you this:
if I can find a way to pay my husband back—   260
your silence.
Woman, on the whole, is a timid thing:
the din of war, the flash of steel, unnerves her;
but, wronged in love,   265
there is no heart more murderous.
LEADER. As you wish, Medea.
You have a score to settle with your lord.
I do not wonder that you smart . . .
But, look, I see Creon coming:
this country's king—
bristling, I dare say, with new decisions.   270
[*enter* CREON *with attendants. He is a bearded man of
about sixty, royally but modestly dressed. His face wears a
look of troubled resolution*]
CREON. Go, Medea. Remove yourself.
Get packing from this land.
I order you—
you with your black-faced fury
lowering against your lord.
And take your brace of offspring with you;
no dallying either.
I am here to see this order done,
and until I've pushed you out and over the border,
I'll not go home.   275
MEDEA. So.
I am lost—crushed utterly.
My enemies let out the sail,
while I have no place to disembark from doom.
Nevertheless, hard-pressed as I am,   280
I ask you this:

For what reason, Creon, do you drive me out?
CREON. Fear:
  no need to camouflage the fact;
  I am afraid you'll deal my child some lethal blow . . .
  and many things conspire to make me fear.
    You are a woman of some knowledge,   285
  versed in many an unsavory skill.
    Your husband's gone:
  your soul is raw with loss of love . . .
  and now it is reported that you threaten me:
  mean to hurt the father of the bride
  and of course the bride and groom.
    That is what I want to guard against—
  an accident.
    Madam, better to be hated now by you   290
  than soften and pay later with regrets.
MEDEA. [*exchanging a look with the* CHORUS] Heaven help me!
  My reputation is a curse:
  This is not the only time it has done me lasting harm.
    Oh, let the perspicacious man
  keep his children from enlightenment—   295
  above the general run.
    It will earn them only
  the sneer of uselessness
  and the spiteful jealousy of fellow men.
    Bring education to the dolt
  and, far from being accounted wise,
  you will yourself be cast as dolt.
    Outshine a pundit of established fame   300
  and you become a byword of distaste.
    This precisely
  is what I have to face.
    Because I have a little knowledge,
  some are filled with jealousy,
  others think me secretive, and crazy.

    In point of fact, my knowledge
  does not amount to much.   305
        [*she turns upon* CREON *eyes pathetic with innocence*]
  But now I frighten *you*:
  do you think I'll strike some death-knell on your house?
    No, no: I am not like that.
    Creon, forget your fear:
  I have no criminal intent against a king.
    For how have *you* wronged me?
    You simply gave your virgin child
  to a suitor of your bent.   310
    No, it is my husband that I hate.
    You, I think, have acted prudently
  and even now I don't begrudge your enterprise success.

Marry them both and blessings on you,
only let me go on living in this land.
      Ill-used though I am, I shall keep quiet:
I am overruled.   315
CREON. Reassuring talk,
but it chills me to the marrow.
      What are you really hatching in your mind?
      I trust you, Madam,
less even than I did before.
      The impassioned woman,
like the impassioned man,
is easier to watch than the crafty and the quiet.   320
      So, leave, I say, at once,
and no speeches, please.
      My mind's made up.
      You are dangerous.
      All your cleverness
shall not keep you here.
MEDEA. Please, I beg you—on my knees—
by your fresh young daughter-bride . . .
CREON. You waste your words.
      I am adamant.   325
MEDEA. Will you expel me—
heedless of my prayers?
CREON. I will. For I love you less
than I love my home.
MEDEA. Ah, home! My own beloved country.
      What memories crowd upon me now!
CREON. Exactly: next to my own children,
my country is *my* dearest love as well.
MEDEA. Love, did you say?   330
      It is a mighty curse.
CREON. In my opinion . . . that depends . . .
MEDEA. O Zeus, remember
the author of this crime.
CREON. Go away—you poor deluded thing—
rid me of my troubles.
MEDEA. The troubles are all mine:
      I have a glut of them.
CREON. [*Turning on his heel*] I'll call the servants:
They'll put you out by force.   335
MEDEA. [*clinging to him*] No, not that . . . Creon,
I have something else . . .
CREON. You seem determined, Madam,
to make a nuisance of yourself.
MEDEA. No, I'll go into banishment . . .
      That is not what I beg you now.
CREON. Then, why not *go*, and let this land be rid of you?
MEDEA. Just let me stay this single day   340
      to arrange my exodus from here

and make provision for my little sons—
whose father cannot bring himself to care.
    Be kind to them.
    You are a father too:
you know what kindly feelings are.   345
    As for me,
it means nothing to me
whether I stay or go.
    It's them I shed my tears for:
their lot is hard.
CREON. [*after a tussle with himself*]
    My soul is not tyrannical enough.
    My heart has often let me down . . .
    So now, Medea,
though I know I take a false step: 350
have it your own way.
    But let me warn you solemnly,
if tomorrow's holy light
sees you and your two children
still inside the borders of this realm,
you die.
    Every word of this I mean.
    Now, stay if you must; but one day only . . .   355
not long enough for you to perpetrate anything I dread.
    [exit CREON]
CHORUS. Ill-starred woman,
    Oh, what a nightmare of anguish is on you!
    Whom will you turn to? Where will you turn?
    What country, what stranger, what home for a haven?   360
        Who will receive you?
    God has certainly steered you—
    Oh, my poor Medea—
    Into a sea-race of sorrows.
MEDEA. [*turning on them with the gleam of revenge*]
    In the center of disasters, yes,
but all is far from lost—make no mistake—   365
a test awaits the newlyweds,
no little ordeal for the happy pair.
    [*with a laugh of derision*]
    Do you think I ever would have toadied to this man
if nothing could be got from it, no gain, no tool?
    No, not one syllable,
not a touch with my little finger.   370
    The fool!
    He could have scotched me with one stroke,
flung me out;
instead he lets me stay one extra day,
to make three enemies three corpses:

ha! father, daughter, and my husband.   375
   [*she leans toward the* CHORUS]
   Friends,
I can think of several ways to bring their death about.
   Which one shall I choose?
   Shall I set their house of honeymoon alight,
or creep into the nuptial bower
and plunge a sharp knife through their vitals?   380
   One thing makes me pause:
   if I am caught entering the palace, or red-handed,
I die . . . and give my enemies the last laugh.
   No, there is a surer way,
one more direct;
for which I have a natural bent:
death by poison.
Yes, that is it.   385
   [*she walks, thinking*]
   Well, suppose they are dead:
will any city take me in,
will any man afford me home in a country safe for living
and shield me from reprisals?
   No, there is none.
   I must postpone it, therefore, for a while
until some tower of strength appears for me;   390
then, through trickery and stealth,
I shall proceed with death by poison
   What if I'm forced to go before it's done?
   Ah, then I shall seize a sword,
face certain death,
and with my own hands run them through.
   I shall not shrink from such a step,   395
by Hecate,[4] no: the goddess who abides
in the shrine of my inner hearth—
the one I reverence most of all the gods
and have chosen to abet me.
   Nobody breaks my heart—
with impunity.
   Their wedding I'll reduce
to agony and grief:
agony for having met and married,
and grief for having banished me.   400
   Good!
   Use your magic to the hilt.
   Plot, Medea, devise your recipes:
advance to the deadly act that tests your courage.
   See your present plight:

---

4. *Hecate*: Identified with Artemis, and sometimes called Persephone (Roman name: Proserpine), she was supposed to preside over magic and witchcraft.

laughed at by the seed of Sisyphus[5]
because of Jason's match? 405
Never.
Your father was a king:
his father, Helios the Sun . . .
be aware of *that*.
Besides, you are a born woman:
feeble when it comes to the sublime,
marvelously inventive over crime.

FIRST CHORAL ODE

[*the* CHORUS *sings an ode about the topsy-turvy changing
standards of the world. Out of the turmoil will come a new
importance for women, and a new reverence. Meanwhile,
Medea is a harbinger of female independence and vitality*]

Back to their fountains   [*Strophe 1*]
   the sacred rivers are falling; 410
The cosmos and all morality
   turning to chaos.
The mind of a man is nothing but fraud
   and his faith in the gods a delusion. 415
One day the story will change:
   then shall the glory
   of women resound,
And reverence will come to the race of woman,
   Reversing at last the sad
   reputation of ladies. 420

The ballads of ages gone by   [*Antistrophe 1*]
   that harped on the falseness
Of women, will cease to be sung . . .
   If only Apollo,
Prince of the lyric, had put
   in *our* hearts the invention
Of music and songs for the lyre, 425
Wouldn't I then have raised
   up a feminine paean
To answer the epic of men?
Time in the roll of the ages has much to unfold
   Of the fortunes of women no less
   than the fortunes of men. 430

So you, Medea, sailing away   [*Strophe 2*]
   from your father's house,
Threading a passage with heart on fire
   through the jowls of the Euxine
Cliffs[6] to inhabit a strange

---

5. *Sisyphus*: To be a descendant of Sisyphus was considered disgraceful by the
ancients.
6. *Euxine Cliffs*: on the Black Sea.

land where your bed is empty of man   435
(The lover you lost, O heartbroken lady!)
Now are chased from the realm,
    shamed and banned.

The joy of a bond is gone;   [*Antistrophe* 2]
    and wide of the world of Hellas,   440
All shame has flown—
    high in the sky and away.
Bereft of a fatherly home,
Where can you sail for a haven against
The storm, unfortunate woman—
    Your bed
Royally quelled by another
    who queens it in your home?   445

Second Episode

[JASON *enters from the road that leads to the palace. He is
a young-looking man, dressed in the swashbuckling cloak
and plumed helmet of a captain in the King's Guards*]
JASON. [*embarrassed and exasperated*]
    So . . . this is not the first time
I have seen irrevocable damage done
by a barbarous rage.
    You could have stayed here,
in this land, in this house,
had you submitted quietly to your ruler's plans.
    Instead, you ranted like a lunatic . . .   450
so now are banished.
    To me your tirade does not mean a thing:
go on declaiming what a monster Jason is.
    But when it comes to royalty,
the princess and the king,
count yourself lucky to be only banished.
    I have tried continuously to calm things down;   455
for I should like you to remain.
    But you, Madam,
obstinate in folly,
have continuously reviled our royalty,
    And so you are banished.
    Yet, in spite of everything, I come, Medea,
patient to the last with someone I am fond of,
to do what I can to help.   460
    You and the children
need not leave the country penniless
and unprovided for . . .
exile drags with it a chain of troubles.
    And hate me though you may,
I cannot bring myself to wish you harm.

MEDEA. You criminal—   465
    an epithet too good for you . . . such inhumanity . . .
    so you come to me, do you,
    you byword of aversion both in heaven and on earth,[7]   468
    to me your own worst enemy?
        This is not courage.
        This is not being brave:
    to look a victim in the eyes whom you've betrayed—   470
    somebody you loved—
        This is a disease,
    and the foulest that a man can have:
    you are shameless.
        [*with the thinnest of smiles*]
    But you have done well to come:
    I can unload some venom from my heart
    and you can smart to hear it.
        To begin at the beginning,   475
    yes, first things first:
        I saved your life—
    as every son of Greece who stepped on board the *Argo* knows.
        You were sent to yoke
    the fire-breathing bulls
    and sow the plot of death.
        Yes, I saved you, lit up life for you,
    when I slew the guardian of the Golden Fleece,
    that giant snake which hugged it, sleepless,   480
    coil on coil.
        I deserted my own father and my home
    to come away with you to Iolcus by Mount Pelion,
    full of zeal and very little sense.   485
        King Pelias, I killed,
    a most horrid death—
    perpetrated through his daughters—
    and overturned their home.
        All this for you,
    I even bore you sons—you most reprobate man—
    just to be discarded for a new bride.
        Had you been childless,   490
    this craving for another bedmate
    might have been forgiven.
        But no: all faith in vows is shattered.
        I am baffled:
        Do you suppose the gods of old no longer rule?
        Or is it that mankind
    now has different principles—
    because your every vow to me, I'm sure you know,   495
    is null and void.
        Curse this right hand of mine,

7. Editors bracket this line as doubtful.

so often held by yours;
and these knees of mine—
sullied to no purpose
by the grasp of a rotten man.
   You turned my hopes to lies.
   Come now, tell me frankly—
as if we were two friends,
as if you really were prepared to help   500
(and I hope the question makes you feel ashamed)—
where do I go from here?
   [*with a bitter laugh*]
   Home to my father, perhaps,
and my native land,
both of whom I sacrificed for *you*?
   Or to the poor deprived daughters of Pelias?
   They would be overjoyed to entertain   505
their father's murderer.
   Yes: this is how things stand.
   Among my own friends
I am an execrated woman.
   There was no call for me to hurt *them*,
but now I have a death-feud on my hands—
and all for you.
   What a reward!
   What a heroine you have made me
among the daughters of Hellas!   510
   Lucky Medea, having *you*:
such a wonderful husband . . . and so loyal!
   I leave this land displaced, expelled,
deprived of friends,
only my children with me, and alone.
   What a charming record for our new bridegroom this:
"His own sons and the wife who saved him   515
are wayside beggars."
   [*she breaks off and looks upward*]
   O Zeus, what made you give us
clear signs for telling
mere glitter from true gold,
but when we need to know
the base metal of a man
no stamp upon his flesh for telling counterfeit?
LEADER. How frightening is resentment   520
      how difficult to cure,
   When lovers hurl past love
      at one another's hate.
JASON. I'll have to choose my words
with no uncommon skill, it seems . . .
like a good sailor riding out a storm,
if I am to sail close-sheeted, Madam,

through your lashing, dangerous tongue.   525
   [*folding his arms*]
   So, you pile up what you did for me
into pinnacles of grace.
   Well, as far as I am concerned,
it was Aphrodite[8] and no one else in heaven or earth
who saved me on my voyage.
   Your cleverness played a part, of course,
but I could underline, if I wanted to be ungenerous,
how it was infatuation, sheer shooting passion,   530
that drove you to save my life.
   I shall not stress the point.
After all, your service did no harm.
   But this I shall maintain:
that what you gained by saving me
was far more than you gave.   535
   [*holds up a hand to stop* MEDEA *from interrupting*]
   In the first place,
you have a home in Hellas
instead of some barbarian land.
   You have known justice:
the benefit of laws which never yield to might;
have had your talents recognized all over Greece
and won renown.
   For, were you living at the world's ends,   540
your name would not be known . . .
   Oh, to me, houses crammed with gold,
and a sweeter song than Orpheus sang,
are nothing with no name.
   But, enough discussion of my dangerous voyage: 545
an argument which *you* provoked.
   Now to your vindictive challenge
of my royal marriage.
   I'll show you, first, it was an act of common sense,
secondly, unselfish,
and, finally, a mark of my devotion
to you and all my family.   550
   [MEDEA *gives a gasp of incredulity*]
   No, be still.
   When I came here from the land of Iolcus,
frustrations crowding on my trail,
could I, a wretched fugitive,
have hit upon a greater stroke of luck
than marriage to the daughter of the king?
   It was not—which cuts you to the quick—
that I was tired of your attractions   555
and smitten with a longing for a new wife;
still less that I was out to multiply my offspring,

---

8. *Aphrodite*: goddess of love, called by the Latins *Venus*.

(I am quite satisfied with the sons we have);
no, it was simply that I wanted above all
to let us live in comfort, not be poor . . .   560
　　I know too well
how the pauper is avoided by his friends.
　　I wanted our children to be reared
in a manner worthy of my ancestry,
and, begetting others, brothers for your sons,
knit them all together
into one close and happy family.
　　What point was there for *you* to have more children?   565
　　My intention was—and it seemed real gain—
to help the ones I have,
through those I hope to have.
　　Was this such a wicked plan?
　　You would not say so,
except through jealousy—that stinging jealousy of bed.
　　You women are all the same.
　　If your love life goes all right,   570
everything is fine;
but once crossed in bed,
the liveliest and best that life can offer
might as well be wormwood.
　　What we poor males really need
is a way of having babies on our own—
no females, please.
　　Then the world would be
completely trouble free.   575
LEADER. [*sternly*] Jason, this speech of yours is plausible,
But say what you like, it is not right
To sacrifice your wife.
MEDEA. [*with cold disdain*]
My outlook must be very different, then, from others.
　　To my mind a hypocrite who is too glib   580
only multiplies the danger that it puts him in:
the more he glozes falsehood with his tongue,
the more confident and rash he grows.
　　He ends by not being very clever.
　　So, you, toward me—
you'd better drop your specious pleading.   585
　　One simple observation
lays the whole thing flat:
were you not a coward, it was your duty
to convince *me*; not go sneaking off to marry.
JASON. And you would have welcomed the suggestion, I am sure.
Why, even now you can't contain your blazing rage.   590
MEDEA. *That* was not what governed you:
you felt your glory tarnished by an aging oriental wife.
JASON. Please, please believe me:

it was nothing to do with women—
my desire to make this match—
but as I have already said   595
to safeguard you and rear young princes
to be brothers to my sons . . .
so make our family solid.
MEDEA. [*with a bitter laugh*]
Haha! Solid happiness on the grave of love;
Prosperity with a secret sting . . .
O you gods—not for me—ever.
JASON. [*earnestly*] Please change your prayer to this   600
and make it reasonable:
    "May success not seem to me sad failure,
nor good fortune ever a disaster."
MEDEA. You go on mocking me: *you* have roof and shelter.
I am deserted, flying for my life, alone.
JASON. *You* chose it. Blame no one else.   605
MEDEA. Did I? I was the one who wed and then betrayed?
JASON. No: you just swore a heap of filthy curses on the king.
MEDEA. Yes, and you shall find that *I* am the curse
that Fate has made to haunt you.
JASON. There's no point in talking any more with you.   610
    [*preparing to go*]
Anything that you or the children want in exile,
let me know; I'd gladly furnish it,
or send letters of introduction for you
to friends abroad who will be kind.
    To turn this offer down, Medea,
is nothing short of madness.
    Forget your feelings of resentment: 615
let yourself be helped.
MEDEA [*spitting out the words*]
Not your friends, not your things:
I would not touch anything of yours—
how dare you offer it!
    The presents of the wicked are pure poison.
JASON. [*flinging his cloak about him*]
In that case, heaven be my witness:
all my design to help you and your sons   620
is thwarted by your preference for evil.
    Your self-will cuts you off.
    Suffer then accordingly.
    [*he begins to go*]
MEDEA. Go then. Don't waste your passion here:
go to the fresh young virgin you can't wait for . . .
Have her.
    [*as* JASON *exits, furious and embarrassed*]
    And God grant   625
the match you make, you'll long to have unmade.

SECOND CHORAL ODE

[*the women of the Chorus, appalled by what has happened to* MEDEA, *speak of the dangers of love and the sufferings of exile*]

Love is a dangerous thing: [*Strophe* 1]
Loving without any limit.
Discredit and loss it can bring . . .
But, oh, if the goddess should visit   630
A love that is modest and right,
No god is so exquisite.
Great lady, aim not at me
Your gold and infallibly
Passion-tipped, poisoned delight.

Stay me with innocent living: [*Antistrophe* 1] 635
Most beautiful gift of the gods.
Never let Cypris[9] the fierce
Queen of desire propel
My heart to a dissolute lust
From old to a new and another
Bed and a dissonant longing,
But test with a sweet eye for peace   640
The love-bonds of reverent women.

O my country, my home, never let   [*Strophe* 2]
Me lose my state and my city—
Living that desperate loss
so helpless and hard, without pity.   645
Death: I would bargain with death,
To die such a day to a finish.
For nothing is like the sorrow
Or supersedes the sadness   650
Of losing your native land.

LEADER. The thing is before my eyes.   [*Antistrophe* 2]
Learned from no rumor or lies:
Medea without city or friends
Nowhere where pity extends—   655
Oh, how you must suffer! . . .
Let a man rot in a charmless lot
If he never unshutters his heart
To the cleansing esteem of another.   660
He'll not be my friend: no, never.

Third Episode

[*enter* AEGEUS *from the country. He is a man in his early middle years and dressed in traveling clothes. His open fea-*

9. *Cypris*: Aphrodite, goddess of love. Roman Venus.

*tures—kindly but unimaginative—seem preoccupied. In his
retinue are* NOBLEMEN *and* SERVANTS]

AEGEUS. [*stretching out his hands*]
Medea, all health and happiness . . .
and one can say a fairer thing when greeting friends?

MEDEA. [*wanly*] Health and happiness to you, good Aegeus,   665
wise Panidon's son . . . But where do you stem from?

AEGEUS. I have just left Apollo's ancient oracle at Delphi.

MEDEA. What—a pilgrim there—the nub of the world of prophecy?

AEGEUS. I went to ask for progeny—for a fruitful seed.

MEDEA. [*suddenly interested*]
In the name of heaven! Have you been childless   670
all this time.

AEGEUS. Childless, yes—by some design of heaven.

MEDEA. But with a wife . . . or have you never married?

AEGEUS. I am married. Yes, I have a wife who shares my bed.

MEDEA. And what did Apollo say about your having children?

AEGEUS. Something far too deep for me, a mere mortal, to unravel. 675

MEDEA. Am I allowed to know the god's reply?

AEGEUS. Certainly. It would take a mind like yours to fathom.

MEDEA. Tell me . . . what did he say . . . since you are allowed?

AEGEUS. Why, just this:
"Do not unstopper the wine-skin till . . ."[1]

MEDEA. Till you've done something—been somewhere—special? 680

AEGEUS. [*baffled*] Until I'm back at home again.

MEDEA. Then why did you sail in here?

AEGEUS. There is a man called Pittheus, king of Troezen . . .

MEDEA. Yes, a son of Pelops: a very pious man, they say.

AEGEUS. I want to ask his help about this oracle.   685

MEDEA. Yes, a clever man, and an expert in such things.

AEGEUS. And of all my old battle cronies, my favorite.

MEDEA. Well, I hope that all your dreams come true.

AEGEUS. Medea, you look so pale, so sad. What is it?

MEDEA. My husband, Aegeus: he is the world's most wicked man. 690

AEGEUS. You don't say? . . . Come, tell me all about your troubles.

MEDEA. He's set up a mistress to queen it in my home.

AEGEUS. Dear me! Would he really do a thing like that?   695

MEDEA. Yes, yes . . . And I am deposed—the one he loved.

AEGEUS. Did he fall in love . . . or is he just tired of *you*?

MEDEA. In love—Ha—head over heels . . . flinging all fidelity to
the winds.

AEGEUS. Let him get on with it . . . since he's as wicked as you say
he is.

MEDEA. But it was with royalty he fell in love: 700
a king's daughter.

AEGEUS. Eh? What king's daughter? Please go on.

1. *"Do not . . . wine-skin"*: probably, "Do not have sexual intercourse."

MEDEA. Creon's, king of Corinth.

AEGEUS. In that case, Madam, it *is* serious.
You have my sympathies.

MEDEA. It is the end. What is more, I am being banished.

AEGEUS. Banished? This is indeed a crowning blow—   705
but by whom?

MEDEA. Creon: he wants to banish me from Corinth.

AEGEUS. And Jason agrees? I find that monstrous.

MEDEA. [*with fierce irony*] Oh, he says he doesn't—
but he'll bear it bravely.

[*on her knees*]
Aegus, I beg you,
by your beard,
by these knees of yours I clasp,   710
pity me, pity my unhappiness.
Do not see me banished and alone,
let me come to Athens, shelter me,
accept me in your home.
The gods will pay you back,
give you the children you so long to have,
surround your death with happiness.   715
You do not guess how Providence has blessed you, meeting
me.
I mean to end your childlessness
and make your seed bear sons.
[*almost in a whisper*]
I promise it. I know the drugs.

AEGEUS. [*impressed*] Medea, many reasons make me ready
to acquiesce in your request,
not least of all the gods;   720
then because you've given me—a promise:
promise of children . . .
oh, left to myself, I had all but given up.
[*gently raising her*]
My proposition, then is this:
get yourself to Athens
and there, as is incumbent on me,
I shall do my utmost to protect you.
However, I must tell you clearly,   725
I cannot take you with me out of Corinth,
but if you reach my palace on your own,
there you shall have full sanctuary
and to no one shall I give you up.
So, by your own means you must leave this land:
I cannot risk offending the Corinthians—
who are also friends of mine.   730

MEDEA. As you say . . . but . . .
if only you could promise it on oath,
it would make it all so . . . settled between us.

AEGEUS. Do you not trust me? What is the matter now?

MEDEA. [*glancing nervously over her shoulders*]
I do trust you . . . but . . .
but I have my enemies.
It isn't only Creon,   735
there is the house of Pelias too:
They'll want to prize me from your territories.
If you are bound by oath
you will not give me up.
But if you have only made a promise,
not sworn it to the gods,
there is always the chance that sheer diplomacy
will win you to their wishes.
I have no weapons on my side,
on theirs is wealth and all the weight of royalty.   740

AEGEUS. You are very provident, Medea.
However, if that is what you want,
I shall not go against it.
In point of fact,
to swear an oath protects me too:
I can counter those who wish you ill
with a clear excuse;
and you of course, are well secured.
So, name your deities.   745

MEDEA. [*in crystal-cold syllables*]
Swear by the Earth on which you tread.
Swear by the Sun, my father's father dread.
Swear by every god and godhead.

AEGEUS. Yes, but what to do or not to do? Please say.

MEDEA. Never yourself to drive me from your land,
and if an enemy of mine tries to drag me off,
never while you live to let me go.   750

AEGEUS. I swear by the Earth and sacred light of the Sun
to abide by the words you have just pronounced.

MEDEA. [*relentlessly*]
Good . . . but if you break your word—what penalty?

AEGEUS. The penalty for sacrilege.   755
[*they clasp hands in silence*]

MEDEA. Go now and be glad. All is well.
I shall come to Athens as quickly as I can,
but first I have some work to do, to carry out a plan.
[*as* AEGEUS *is leaving*]

LEADER. We hope that Hermes, master of journeys,
Will hasten you home safely to Athens: 760
Home to the hope of your heart's desire,
For, Aegeus, you are
A most magnanimous man.

MEDEA. [*wheels round and faces the* CHORUS]
O Zeus and lady daughter, Justice,

O resplendent Sun!
And you my friends,   765
    At last we are on the road to vengeance
and to our song of triumph. At last there is hope:
we shall see my enemies put down.
    At the very point my plot could founder,
this man opens up a port, an anchorage.   770
    So to Athens I shall go
and moor to her fast towers.
    [*she beckons the women closer*]
    Now I can unfold to you my whole design:
there is nothing sweet in it, as you will see.
    I send a servant of my house to Jason
asking him to come to me.   775
    He arrives
I tell him in the softest accents;
how I now agree;
how it all seems for the best:
his royal marriage, his sacrifice of me;
everything that he has planned is for the best.
    But I ask him to let my children stay . . .   780
with no intention—you understand—
of leaving any child of mine in a hostile place
for those who hate me to maltreat.
    No, this is just a device
for murdering the daughter of the king.
    I send them there with presents in their hands,
presents for the bride—as a kind of plea   785
against their banishment—
yes, a gown of gossamer and a diadem made of beaten gold.
    If she takes this finery and puts it on,
the girl will die in agony
and anyone who touches her;
so deadly are the poisons I shall steep the presents in.
    But now my whole tone changes: 790
a sob of pain for the next thing I must do.
    I kill my sons—my own—
no one shall snatch them from me.
    And when I have desolated Jason's house beyond recall,
I shall escape from here:
fly from the murder of my little ones,   795
my mission done.
    People that one hates, my friends,
must never have the last laugh.
    Well, so be it.
    What good is life to me?
    I have no father, home, defense from danger.
    Oh, the mistake I made was when I left his house,   800
trusting the word of a man from Greece . . .

but he is going to pay the price.
    Never again alive
shall he see the sons he had by me,
nor any child by this new bride of his—
poor girl, who has to die a wretched death,   805
poisoned by me.
    Let no man think me insignificant or weak:
I am no meek martyr, no—quite the contrary—
relentless an enemy I make;
though kind enough to friends.
    Such is the genius of my life.   810
LEADER. [*imploringly*]
Though you have shared all this in confidence with us, Medea,
and though I long to be of help,
we must uphold the laws of life:
and so I say to you: "You must not do it."
MEDEA. There is no other way.
And though I understand your sentiments,
you have not been through my agony.   815
LEADER. But, my lady, to kill your own two sons . . .?
MEDEA. It is the supreme way to hurt my husband.
LEADER. And it makes you the most desolate of women.
MEDEA. Be that as it may.
Argument is now superfluous.
    [*she turns to the* NURSE, *who has entered during the pre-
    vious dialogue*]
Nurse, when I need real loyalty
you are the one I always turn to.
Go now and fetch Jason here.   820
    But as you are a woman
and a faithful servant of this house,
whisper no syllable of what I plan.
    [*exit* NURSE, *dragging her feet*]

THIRD CHORAL ODE

    [*the* WOMEN *of Corinth desperately try to move* MEDEA
    *from her purpose. Does she imagine Athens, that blessed
    land, will welcome a murderess? Surely, she herself will
    flinch from the cold-blooded killing of her sons?*]

The people of Athens are blest through the ages, [*Strophe 1*] 825
    Seeds of the all-hallowed gods,
Born on a soil unravaged and holy,
    They feed on the wide
    Bright pastures of knowledge.
Lightly they walk through the crystal air   830
In a land where Harmonia,
    Goldenly fair,

Once gave birth, they say, to the nine
 Muses, the pure
 Maids of Pieria.²

And out of the sweetly flowing currents   [*Antistrophe* 1] 835
 Of Cephisus,³ they declare,
Aphrodite sprinkles the land
 And fragrantly breathes
 Delicate breezes.
Forever she sheds from the stream of her hair,   840
 Plaited with roses,
Scented petals; and sends the Loves—the Erotes—
To preside with Wisdom over the heart
 And together prepare
 The glories of art.   845

How then shall a glorious city,   [*Strophe* 2]
 City of sacred rivers,
 Host of the salutary guest,
Kindly take to the killer of children,
Harbor among them a murderess?   850
Think of how you are stabbing your sons.
Think, too, of the blood you assume.
Do not, please, we beg by your knees,
By everything and every means—
 Murder your children.   855

Where, when, will you find the mind,   [*Antistrophe* 2]
 The hand or the callous heart
 Hardened enough to strike
These, yours—oh, heartless enough?—
How then will you see through your gaze   860
Swollen with tears as you sight your aim?
No, no, when your little ones kneel
Crying for mercy, yóu will nót
Find the nerve, never be able,
 To bloody your hands.   865

Fourth Episode

[JASON *enters with the* NURSE *behind him. On his face is
written apprehension mixed with hope; on hers, despair*]
JASON. I have come, Medea, because you asked me.
 I put myself at your disposal
even though you are against me.
 What, Madam, can I do for you?
MEDEA. [*in a small, contrite voice*]
 Jason please forgive me for all the things I said.   870

2. *Where Harmonia . . . Maids of Pieria*:
Harmonia, the balance of nature, and
the genius of the people resulted in the
cultivation of the arts. Pieria was a holy
fountain in Boetia where the nine Muses
were supposed to live.
3. *Cephisus*: an Athenian river.

Bear lightly with my outbursts, will you,
if only in remembrance of our great love together.
I have been arguing with myself,
have taxed myself severely.
"You raving fool," I said,
"To antagonize those who want to do you good,
setting yourself against your rulers and your husband.   875
His royal marriage
and his design to bring up brothers for your sons
does you the greatest service that he could.
Why not calm yourself?
Are *you* suffering because the gods are good?
Have you no children of your own?   880
And are you not aware
you came as fugitive with not too many friends?"
Such reflections made me realize
I have been out of my mind, hysterical.
Now I thank you.
Now I am convinced
that in securing us this benefit   885
you are the wise one, *I* the fool—
I who should have been your ally
and encouraged you.
Yes, I should have been at hand to help,
decked the bed, dressed the bride—
and been glad to do it . . .
But we women—
well, we are what we are: let's leave it at that!
Do not copy us in our perverseness   890
or try to get your own back, giving tit for tat.
I ask your pardon.
I admit to being wrong.
I've thought better of it now.
   [*with an upsurge of put-on happiness*]
Children, children, come out here,
out of the house.
   [*the two* BOYS *appear with their* TUTOR]
Come greet your father, hug him, join with me   895
in loving, not resenting him.
Your mother's rancor's over.
There's peace between us: the fighting's done.
Come, take his hand.
   [*as the children run into their father's arms*]
O God, what a presentiment!
What an image looming in the dark!   900
JASON. My sons, my sons,[4]

4. To my mind there is no doubt that this line and half the next (in the Greek) go to Jason, and not Medea as the manuscripts and editors have it. Otherwise, Medea's remark in 930 makes no sense. The attempt to have it correspond to Jason's wish in 916 does not work.

if only you could go on living, go on loving,
with your arms stretched out like that to me forever . . .
MEDEA [*choking*] It breaks my heart;
I am far too prone to tears, too full of tears . . .
it is the sudden ending of my quarrel with your father
which makes them flow.
A sight so touching . . .
it overflows.   905
LEADER. My eyes, too, are stinging,
but may this be the worst that is to come.
JASON. [*gently releasing the* BOYS] I praise you now, Medea,
and I did not blame you then.
It is natural for a woman to be enraged
when her husband goes off making second marriages.   910
But now
you are in a better frame of mind
and, even if it took a little time,
realize the good points of this plan . . .
the decision is a level-headed woman's.
[*turning to the children*]
As for you, my boys,
your father has been far from idle
and, heaven willing, he has made
good settlements for you.   915
In time I shouldn't wonder
if you were not first citizens in Corinth—
along with your new brothers.
[*laying his hands on their shoulders*]
Grow up now fine fellows.
Your father and a kindly providence
have the rest in hand.   920
How I look toward the time
when you will be two strapping grown young men,
trampling down my enemies.
[MEDEA *has averted her head and is sobbing. Her feelings,
though genuine, are being used by her to further her next
move*]
But, Medea, what is this—
these dewy eyes, these tears;
your white face turned away
as if my words struck pain, not joy?   925
MEDEA. It is nothing.
I was just thinking of our sons.
JASON. Well, be of good heart now:
I shall see them through.
MEDEA. I will do my best . . . it isn't that I don't believe you,
but you know how women weep.
JASON. I know, but don't be sad for *them* . . . why should you?
MEDEA. [*watching the tender look on* JASON's *face*]

I am their mother.
When you prayed just now   930
for a long life for your sons,
a sudden sadness whispered: "Will this be?"
    Well, that's one item only
of what I had to say.
    The other thing is this:
Since the king has set his mind
on sending me away from Corinth,
and since I've come to recognize that this is best   935
(for I'd only be an obstacle to you,
living with the royal family here—
who think I am a menace to their house),
I shall take myself away, go into banishment.
    But the children, please, I should like *them*
to grow up under your own hand.
    Persuade Creon to let them stay.   940
JASON. [*taken off his guard, but flattered*]
    I—I am not certain that I can:
it'll take a little trying.
MEDEA. But you could ask your wife to beg her father
to let the two boys stay.
JASON. [*reflecting*] Why not? I think I can get her to agree.
MEDEA. Of course you can:
if she's the slightest bit like any woman.   945
    And here *I* can play a useful part.
    I shall send her a present
more ravishingly beautiful, believe me,
than anything this age has seen:
a gown of gossamer and a diadem of beaten gold.
    These the boys shall carry them to her.   950
    [*she claps her hands and two* MAIDS *appear*]
Go quickly, one of you,
and bring the gorgeous presents here.
    [*one of the* MAIDS *hurries into the house*]
What a double delight
What a shower of happiness for her
to have you for a hero husband
and now these treasures which were handed down
by my father's father—the glorious Sun.   955
    [*the* MAID *comes back with two boxes.* MEDEA *turns to the*
    BOYS]
Boys, take hold of this wedding gift.
Carry it to the happy princess-bride.
Place it in her hands.
It is not the kind of present she'll despise.
JASON. [*as the* BOYS *step forward*]
    You foolish woman—why empty your hands?
Do you think a royal wardrobe is in want,   960

or a palace short of gold?
    Keep these things. Don't give them up.
    If my wife values me at all,
my mere wish will have more weight than *things*,
I'm sure of that.
MEDEA. [*with an onrush of conviction*] Do not deny me.
    Even the gods, they say, succumb to gifts,
and gold is stronger than the strongest wits.   965
    She is lucky, *she* is blessed, *she* increases.
    This exile I would barter for my babies
not just with gold but with my life.
    [*forcing the boxes into the* BOYS' *hands*]
    Go, my sons, into the halls of wealth;
down on your knees and beg her—
this new wife of your father's, and my mistress—   970
to let you stay in Corinth.
    Most important of all,
see that she takes the precious things
into her own hands.
    [*packing them off*]
    Quick, now, go. Success be yours.
    Come and tell me the good news.   975
    Your mother waits with all ears.
    [*exeunt the* BOYS *with their* TUTOR, *followed by* JASON]

FOURTH CHORAL ODE

[*the multimurders are imminent. Woe to the victims! Woe
to the murderess!*]

Now has the last hope gone of the children living,   [*Strophe 1*]
Gone and forever: they walk already to murder.
The bride is taking the golden diadem,
    Is taking the poison and doom.
Over her yellow hair her hands are fitting
    The decorated dying.   980

The gorgeousness of the gossamer gown will win, [*Antistrophe 1*]
And the beaten gold of the diadem embrace her.
The bride is decked and ready to meet the dead.   985
    The trap is lethally set:
Doomed miserable woman, doomed to fall in—
    Ineluctably caught by Fate.

And you who are groomed for a murder: [*Strophe 2*]   990
    Son-in-law of a king,
    Jason unsuspecting—
Are to bring on your sons a demise, and a death
    On your bride of a hideous kind.
      Unhappy man, how far
      You are falling.   995

And you the unenviable mother,   [*Antistrophe 2*]
  How I weep for your pain!
  Killer of children for
A vengeance of love that has gone, betrayed   1000
By your man for another
Bride whom he sleeps beside
  In his wrong.

Fifth Episode

[*the* TUTOR *hurries in from the palace with the two* BOYS]
TUTOR. [*breathless with excitement*] My lady, your boys—
they won't be banished.
  And the princess, the bride—
  with her own hands—
  she took your presents, oh, so gladly . . .
  Now the children's danger is over!   1005
    [*baffled by* MEDEA'S *grim reaction*]
  Well I never! Isn't this good news?
  What so transfixes you?
    [MEDEA *draws in her breath in a muffled cry of pain*]
TUTOR. What I hear is out of tune with what I say.
    [MEDIA *sighs deeply*]
TUTOR. I thought I brought good news.   1010
  What kind of news, I wonder, have I brought?
MEDEA. What you have brought, you have brought:
  the fault is not with you.
TUTOR. Why, my Lady, these shuttered eyes:
  these tears falling?
MEDEA. Oh, I am pressed, old friend—hard pressed:
  the gods and my own evil counsels.
TUTOR. Courage, dear mistress: 1015
  Your sons will always bring you home.
MEDEA. [*in a kind of trance*]
  Home? . . . First I must send others there . . . Mercy!
TUTOR. You are not the only mother to be severed from her sons.
  We have to bear our own humanity—humanely.
MEDEA. [*pressing his hand*]
  I shall try . . . Now go inside
  and see what the children need today.   1020
    [*exit* TUTOR, *worried*]
MEDEA. [*throwing out her arms toward the two* BOYS]
  My sons, my sons,
  you will have a city and a home
  far from me.
  I shall be left lonely,
  and you will live without your mother always.
  For I must go in exile to another land:
  never have my joy in you,

or see your bright young progress;   1025
never deck your brides, your marriage beds,
or light you radiant to your wedding day.
      [*the* BOYS *are now in her arms*]
   Oh, what a blight my ruthlessness has been!
   How useless, little ones,
my nursing all your growing up!
   How useless all the cares endured: 1030
the wearying solicitudes,
the shooting agony of giving you your lives.
   And now, how miserably have dwindled
my innumerable dreams of you:
your loving comfort when I'm old,
your own hands dressing me when I am dead—
a passing every person might desire.   1035
   Such sweet fancy vanishes
and, wrenched from you instead,
I shall drag my sad life out alone.
      [*she cups their faces in her hands in turn*]
   Your own dear eyes shall miss forever
your poor mother's face—
your way of life and hers utterly apart.
   Oh, children,
do you let those eyes now stare their fill,   1040
and your last smiles linger to the last?
      [*she turns to the* CHORUS, *panting*]
   O–h! What shall I do?
   My heart dissolves
when I gaze into their bright irises . . .
   No, I cannot do it.
   Goodbye to my determination.
   I shall take my boys away with me.   1045
   Why damage *them* in trying to hurt their father,
and only hurt myself twice over?
   No, I cannot.
   Goodbye to my decisions.
      [*a pause, then she suddenly breaks away from the* BOYS]
   What—what undermines me now?
   Do I really mean to let my enemies go,   1050
to laugh at me?
   Steel yourself, Medea:
away with this cowardice, these arguments that melt.
      [*almost pushing them*]
Go, Boys, into the house.
      [*she turns to the* CHORUS *grimly*]
   Anyone whose conscience will not let him stay
let him look to it: avoid my sacrifice . . .
this hand of mine shall never falter.   1055
      [*another spasm of emotion grips her, and she runs to the*

BOYS *as they reach the door*]
No, no! Stop me, my heart:
we must not do this thing.
    Let them go, you stricken woman,
spare your sons.
    Let them live with you in Athens:
they will be your joy.
    [*throwing her arms round them again*]
    Ah! Not by all the haunting spirits of the underworld,
shall I leave my children for my enemies to trample down.
No, never.[5]   1060
    [*with a sharp realization*]
    But—they have to die—
the whole thing is settled anyway . . .
    Yes . . . the diadem is on her head . . .   1065
the royal bride at this moment rots,
dying in her gown—I know it.
    [*she turns to the* CHORUS *as if to explain her second impulsive embrace*]
You see: the path I have to tread
is unutterably sad,
but the one I set these children on
is sadder still . . .
    Therefore I desire to speak with them.
    [*seizing their hands*]
    Give me your right hands to kiss,
each of you, my little ones—
give them to your mother.   1070
    [*covering their hands, their faces, their bodies, in kisses*]
    How adorable—this hand—and this . . .
These lips—how very much adored!
And this face and form of childhood's
ingenuous nobility . . . how I bless you both . . .
not here—beyond . . .
every blessing here your father has despoiled.
    So sweet . . . the mere touch of you: 1075
the bloom of children's skin—so soft . . .
their breath—a perfect balm.
    [*gently releasing them; then almost savagely turning her back*]
    Go, go . . . I cannot look at you.
I am in an agony, and lost.
    [*the two* BOYS, *weeping, hurry into the house*]
    The evil that I do, I understand full well,
But a passion drives me greater than my will.
    Passion is the curse of man:
It wreaks the greatest ill.   1080

5. Some editors omit lines 1062 and 1063 as a melodramatic interpolation: "But they have to die, and since they must,/ let it be by the hands of her who gave them life."

FIFTH CHORAL ODE

[if there can be a feminine philosophy of parenthood, is its
honest judgment likely to be that children are worth it after
all?]

    So often before
Have I gone toward concepts far too tenuous
And come upon questions far too deep
For the race of woman to try to unravel.
Nevertheless, even we women
Have a muse of our own, that ushers us in.   1085
(Though, alas, not all) to the world of wisdom.
Perhaps you might find it one in a thousand.
It serves to inspire the talent of ladies,
And makes me able now to proclaim   1090
That people without the function of parent
Are happier than begetters of offspring.
The childless man has no way of telling
Whether he misses a curse or a blessing.   1095
Nevertheless, the childless person
Certainly misses many a burden.
I mark how the man with children growing
Sweetly at home is worn with worrying: 1100
How to make sure they are properly fed,
How to leave them a livelihood.
And then after all to be in the dark:
Were all the worries worth it or not?
Were they a worthy or worthless lot?   1105

    But now let me tell
Of the worst and saddest trait of all.
Suppose the children have quite a good life,
Reach their teenhood honest and fine,   1110
What if a fate like Death the cruel
Carries them downward body and soul?
What is the use if after all
(On top of all those other ones)
The gods let loose this grief as well . . .   1115
Just for the joy of having sons?

Sixth Episode

*[*MEDEA *has been sitting during the Chorus. Now she leaps*
up as she catches sight of a man lunging breathlessly to-
ward them from the street: the MESSENGER*]*

MEDEA: Somebody with news at last, my friends,
    And from the right direction.
      Yes, I see him:
    one of Jason's men—panting as he hurries—

With some tremendous news of bad.   1120
> [*the* MESSENGER—*an official of the Bride's house—bursts in:
> hardly able to get his words out*]

MESSENGER. Run, Medea, run!
What—you have done . . . is . . . too unthinkable . . .
too awful . . .
Seize whatever means you can . . .
sailing boat or chariot . . . Escape!

MEDEA. Run? Escape? Is it then so vital?

MESSENGER. Dead . . . They are this minute dead . . .
the princess royal with her father—
and through your poisons.   1125

MEDEA. What a pretty word you bring—
my benefactor, my friend forever!

MESSENGER. [*recoiling*] What are you saying, Madam?
Are you in your right mind—not unhinged?
A king's home a charnel house—   1130
and you rejoice? . . . Are you not afraid?

MEDEA. I have my ready answer too,
so don't be hasty, friend,
but tell me how they perished.
An appalling death
would give me double joy.   1135

MESSENGER. [*supports himself against a pillar as he begins to recol-
lect an agonizing experience*]
We were so pleased to see your brace of boys
come hand in hand to the bride's house with their father:
for your ordeal had upset us servants greatly.
The rumor went racing through the house
that all was well again between your husband and yourself.   1140
Some of us kissed the children's hands,
kissed their golden tops;
and I in my enthusiasm even followed them
to the women's wing.
There, the mistress—
I mean the one we have to honor now—
had eyes so taken up with Jason
she did not even see at first   1145
the two boys hand in hand.
But when she did,
a veil of scorn dropped over her eyes,
she turned her lovely face away,
bristling at your sons' intrusion.
Your husband then began to woo her
from her petulance and girlish tantrums, saying: 1150
"You must not hate your friends.
Stop being hurt and turn your head around.
Consider yours your husband's loved ones.
Come, won't you take their presents

and beseech your father
to let these boys off banishment—just for me?"   1155
[*pauses and sits down hopelessly on a step*]
When she saw how exquisite the presents were,
far from holding out on him,
there was nothing she withheld:
but gave in completely to her groom.
And hardly had your husband and your children
left the house
when she took the gorgeous robe and put it on,
and placed the golden circlet on her curls,   1160
arranging the ringlets in the brightness of a mirror
and smiling at her own dead image there.
Then rising from her stool
she minced off through the halls
on dainty milk white toes,
wildly pleased with what she had received,   1165
over and over again
running her eyes down the clear sweep to her heels.
But all at once
a hideous spectacle took place.
Her color changed. She tottered back;
shuddered in every limb; was able just in time
to fall into a chair and not upon the floor.   1170
An old woman there, attending her,
thinking that perhaps the fierce possession of Pan[6]
or some other power was on her,
broke into a chant of wonder,
then saw the white froth spuming at her lips,
her eyeballs bulging all askew,
her skin quite leached of blood,   1175
and changed her chanting to a yelp:
a wail of horror.
A maid went dashing to the palace for her father,
another went to tell the fresh-wed groom
what was happening to his bride.
The whole house rang with footsteps running.   1180
It took no longer than a sprinter takes
to go the hundred yards,
before the poor girl lay unconscious with her eyelids shut.
Then suddenly she rallied
and gave a curdling shriek,
fighting off a double nightmare.   1185
[*he pauses, gulps, takes a deep breath*]
The golden diadem that clasped her head
burst into a voracious and uncanny flow of fire,
while the robe of gossamer your children gave her

6. Pan, the god of wild nature, who was   sudden madness. Hence, "panic."
supposed to be the cause of seizures and

began to eat her tender flesh away.
　Streaming with flame,
she leapt up from her chair and fled,　　　　　　　　1190
tossing her mane of hair from side to side,
in a frantic bid to shake the diadem off.
　But its grip was adamant
and the golden circlet held.
　The more she tossed,
the more the fire flowed,
till, overwhelmed with pain,　　　　　　　　　　　1195
she sank down to the floor—
unrecognizable to all except her father—
her calm regard grotesquely twisted,
her sweet symmetry all shattered;
and from the crown of her head in molten clots
fire and blood dripped down together.
　The flesh curdled off her bones　　　　　　　　1200
like the teardrops congealing out of pines,
inexplicably dissolved by those ravening venoms.
　It was curious and horrible to see.
　No one dared to touch her body:
the warning was too obvious.
　But her father, unawares, poor man,
rushed headlong through the room,　　　　　　　1205
flung himself lamenting on the body,
hugged and kissed it, sobbing out:
　"My stricken darling,
what evil power has done this to you,
who has made you dead
and left me, like some ancient tombstone, derelict?
O gods! . . . let me die with you, my daughter."　　　1210
　But . . . but when he stopped . . .
from these outpourings—
these melancholy sobs . . .
and tried to lift his aged carcass up,
he found himself stuck fast—
clamped to the flimsy robe
like ivy to a laurel bole.
　A ghastly wrestling match ensued.
　He would try to raise a knee,　　　　　　　　1215
she would drag him back;
and when he took to force,
his own decrepit flesh
pulled off from the bone.
　At last, exhausted,
pathetically unable
to lift himself above the shambles,
he gave his spirit up.
　There they lie, corpse by corpse,　　　　　　　1220

father and young daughter—
fit objects for our tears.
      [*he rises, swaying*]
      To you, Medea . . . from me . . .
there are no words to say.
      Retribution? You yourself will know
the best escape . . .
though in my esteem—and not just for today—
the whole of life is shadow,
and I would even say: 1225
the people who know best or seem to know,
the subtlest professors,
are the very ones who pay the dearest price.
      [*flinging his cloak about him*]
      A happy human being? Ha, there's no such thing . . .
more prosperity, more success in one maybe:
but happier? . . . It does not make one happy.   1230
      [*exit* MESSENGER]
LEADER. Justice personified this day
has brought on Jason's head
— oh, we have seen it!—
the richest retribution.
      But it is you we weep for,
poor blighted child of Creon,
walking through the gates of death
because you married Jason.   1235
MEDEA. [*in clear, cold tones*]
      Now, friends, to complete this mission with dispatch:
to slay my children and hurry from this land.
      I must not dawdle and betray my sons
to much more savage hands than mine to kill.
      There's no way out. They have to die.   1240
      And since they must,
let me be the one to cut them down:
the very one who gave them life!
      [*she begins her walk to the door, almost like a sleepwalker,
      talking to herself*]
      Yes, heart, be steel.
      Why vacillate?
      The act is . . .
necessary as it is cruel and hard.
      Come, reluctant hand,
grip the sword—grip it, Medea:
cross your borderline of lifelong pain.   1245
      Away this flinching!
      Away this longing:
consign to oblivion the love you had for them—
the children of your flesh.
      Even when you kill them they are dear . . .

oh, my sons! . . . I am in despair, despair.   1250
     [MEDEA, *with the* NURSE *mutely following in tears, passes
     into the house*]

SIXTH CHORAL ODE

[*the women pray desperately for something to stop the
imminent murder*]

Come Earth, come sunshafts of the Sun,   [*Strophe*]
Behond this woman and withhold her
From her laying scarlet fingers
On the children of her blood.
Gold of your gold are they begotten: 1255
Heinous is to spill this holy
Ichor in the blood of mortals.
Curb her, stop her, godborn Light, oh,
Keep this house from murder! Keep it
Never haunted by the Furies.[7]   1260

Were those birth pangs wasted bearing: [*Antistróphe*]
Children's birth pangs wasted birth?
You, my lady, after sailing
Safe between the dark blue clashing
Gorges, will you hug a rankling   1265
Hatred to your heart, a loathsome
Rage for murder and revenge?
Those that spill the blood of family
Stain themselves with heaven's anger,
Haunt their homes with doom forever.   1270

Seventh Episode or Denouement

     [*cries are heard from inside the house*]
FIRST WOMAN. A shout—listen—a shout from the boys.
FIRST BOY. O–h! What can we do? . . .
     Our mother is on us!
SECOND BOY. Brother, brother! . . . We're going to be killed.
SECOND WOMAN. That murderous relentless woman!
THIRD WOMAN. Shall we break in, snatch them from death?   1275
FIRST BOY. Yes, by heaven . . . save us . . . help!
SECOND BOY. We're trapped, cornered . . . now . . . by her sword.
     [*as the* CHORUS *beat on the barred doors, there are groans
     and cries, and presently a trickle of blood oozes from under
     the doors. The women watch it, fascinated*]
CHORUS. Woman of stone, heart of iron,
     Disconsolate woman, ready to kill   1280
     The seed of your hands with the hand that tilled.

7. *Furies*: ministers of the vengeance of   guilty on earth as well as in the under-
the gods, employed in punishing the   world.

One other only, one have I known
Murderously handle the fruit of her womb:
Ino the maniac, god-driven one,
Whom Zeus's wife drove out to roam—[8]
Desperate woman goaded to slaughter   1285
The sons of her flesh, clean against nature.
She pitched from the precipice into the sea,
Fell where her foot fell into the ocean,
Dashing two infants to death with her own.   1290
What ghastlier thing is left to be known?

Women, O women, in love and in pangs,
What ruin you've brought on us human beings!
        [JASON, *breathless, his face twisted with hatred, bursts in
        with a troop of servants*]
JASON. You women standing here outside this house,
is that she-ravager, Medea, still at home,   1295
or has she fled?
        [*he waits for a reply, but the women cower before the
        door*]
Deep down in the earth let that woman hide,
or wing into the highest alcoves of the sky,
before she ever saves herself from justice by this royal house.
        Does she think that she can kill
a princess and a country's king
and vanish with impunity?   1300
        [*he strides toward the door*]
But it is my sons, not her, I fear for.
She, she shall be repaid
through her victims.
        I have come to save my children's lives
from some enormous retribution by the family of the dead
for those enormities their mother did.   1305
LEADER. Jason, you poor optimistic man,
you still don't know the evils that have come—
or you would not say what you have said.
JASON. What? Does she mean to kill me too?
LEADER. Your sons are dead: murdered by their mother.
JASON. [*reeling*] What—did—you—say?
Oh, woman—my own wife—you kill me too.   1310
LEADER. [*as the women form an avenue to the door, and* JASON
        *sees for the first time the blood beginning to trickle down
        the steps*]
        Yes. Your children.
You cannot think of them as being alive.

---

8. *Ino the maniac . . . out to roam:* Ino, a daughter of Cadmus and Harmonia, tried to destroy her two stepchildren so that her own two children might ascend the throne. Pursued, in turn, by their father, her husband Athamas, she leapt into the sea with her two boys. This is Euripides' version.

JASON. [*limply*]
    Where did she kill them . . . here . . . outside,
    or was it in the house?
LEADER. Force these doors
    and you will see your children in their blood.
JASON. [*drawing his sword in a frenzy*] Servants, on the double,
    break these bolts,
    force the hinges: let me see   1315
    the double homicide,
    the murdered dead . . . and the murderess to die.
        [*there is a rumbling sound, and out of a cloud above the
        house* MEDEA *appears in a chariot drawn by dragons. By her
        side are the dead bodies of the two* BOYS]⁹
MEDEA. [*in triumphant disdain*]
    Why this battering, this beating at the doors?
    Are you looking for their bodies—
    and for me who did this thing?
    Save yourself the trouble.
    If there's anything you want, then ask.   1320
    But me you shall not lay a hand upon.
    This chariot, the Sun
    —my father's father—gave me
    to keep me safe against my enemies.
JASON. [*hissing with revulsion*]
    You miserable, mephitic woman!
    Beyond abhorrence—
    by me, the gods, the rest of men—
    you could put your own sons to the sword,   1325
    the sons you bore,
    and kill me too with childlessness . . .
    Yet still look upon the sun, see the earth . . .
    Be damned! . . .
    At last I understand
    what I never understood before,
    when I took you from your foreign home to live in Greece,   1330
    the sheer wickedness of you,
    the treachery to your father and the land that reared you.
    You are possessed
    and the gods have unleashed the fiend in you on *me*;
    on your own brother, too, cut down in his home
    before you came aboard the sweet ship *Argo*'s hull.   1335
    Your work already had begun.
    You married me, bore my sons,
    and murdered them through jealousy of love.
    No woman in the whole of Hellas
    would have dared so much;   1340
    yet you were the one I married,

---

9. Euripides was a past master at theatrical effects. He loved *ex machina* contrivances.

not a girl from Greece.
   Oh, I married a tigress,
not a woman, not a wife,
and yoked myself to a hater and destroyer:
to a viciousness more fierce than any Tuscan Scylla.[1]
   [*turning away from the door in a gesture of helplessness*]
   But why go on?
A million accusations would not make you wince:
you are shameless through and through . . .   1345
you—you bloodstained ogress, infanticide . . .
   Hell take you!
   Leave me to mourn my destiny of pain:
my fresh young wedding without joy,
my sons begot and reared and lost—
never to be seen alive again.   1350
MEDEA. [*with acid imperiousness from the chariot*] How tediously
   I could rebut you point by point!
   Zeus the Father knows
exactly what you got from me
and how you then behaved.
   I would not let you or your royal princess
set our wedded life aside,
make me cheap,
so that you could live in bliss;   1355
or let that match-arranger, Creon,
dismiss me from the land without a fight.
   So, call me a tigress if you like,
or a Scylla haunting the Tyrrhenian shore,
I have done what I ought:
broken your own heart to the core.   1360
JASON. [*wheeling round to face her*]
   You are in agony too:
you share my broken life.
MEDEA. It is worth the suffering
       since *you* cannot scoff.
JASON. Poor children, what a monster
       fate gave you for a mother!
MEDEA. Poor sons, what a disaster
       your selfish father was!
JASON. It was not *his* right hand
       that killed and struck them down.   1365
MEDEA. No, it was his pride:
       the lust of his new love.
JASON. You think it right to murder
       just for a thwarted bed.
MEDEA. And do you think that a thwarted bed
       is trifling to a woman?

---

1. *Tuscan Scylla*: a monster that inhabited the straits between Italy and Sicily and snatched sailors off passing ships and devoured them.

JASON. A modest woman, yes:
> to you the world's worst crime.

MEDEA. [*pointing at the dead children*]
See, they are no more:
> I can hurt you too.   1370

JASON. They'll live, I think,
> in your tormented brain.

MEDEA. The gods know who began
> this whole calamity.

JASON. Yes, the gods know well
> your pernicious heart.

MEDEA. Hate then: I spurn
> the wormwood from your lips.

JASON. As I do yours; so let us
> be rid of one another.   1375

MEDEA. Yes, but on what terms?
> That's also what *I* want.

JASON. Let me have the boys—
> to mourn and bury them.

MEDEA. Never!
My own hands shall bury them, they shall be carried
to the sanctuary of Hera on the Cape,
where no enemy shall ever do them harm   1380
or violate their sepulchre.

Here in Corinth, the land of Sisyphus,
I shall inaugurate a solemn festival[2]
with rites in perpetuity
to exorcise this murder.

I myself shall go to Athens, land of Erechtheus,
to live with Aegeus, Pandion's son . . .   1385
you to a paltry death that fits you well:
your skull smashed by a fragment of the *Argo*'s hull:
ironic ending to the saga of your love for me.

The Exodos

[*as the* CHORUS *begin to form for the exodos march, the
meter changes.[3]* JASON *strides into the middle of the arena*]

JASON. Murder is punished, and you'll be destroyed
> by the avenging phantoms of your children.   1390

MEDEA. What power or divine one is ready to hear you:
> perjurer, liar, treacherous guest?

JASON. Vile, vile, murderess of little ones!

MEDEA. Go—go and bury your bride.

JASON. Broken I go: bereft of two sons.   1395

MEDEA. You bemoan too soon: wait till you're old.

JASON. Dearest children!

---

2. *Solemn festival:* similar ceremonies
were still performed at Corinth in Euripides' time.
3. To anapests and dactyls.

MEDEA.   Dear to their mother.

JASON. And so she slew them.

MEDEA.   To get at your heart.

JASON. You did! You did! How I long to press
my little children's lips to mine!   1400

MEDEA. Now you are longing, now you call;
you utterly turned from them before.

JASON. For the love of the gods, allow me this:
to stroke my children's tender skin.

MEDEA. No, you shall not: you waste your words.

JASON. [*flinging out his arms*] Zeus, do you hear how I'm at bay,   1405
Dismissed by this ogress, odious woman,
Tigress besmirched with the blood of her young?
So I mourn and call on the gods while I may,
On the powers to witness how you have slain   1410
My children, and now prevent my hands
From touching them, dead, interring their clay.
I'd rather they'd never been born to me
Than have lived to see you destroy them this day.

> [*before the end of these words,* MEDEA, *with a cold, vindic-
> tive smile, has moved off in the chariot.* JASON *staggers out
> of the arena*]

Envoi

CHORUS. Wide is the range of Zeus on Olympus.   1415
Wide the surprise which the gods can bring:
What was expected is never perfected,
What was not, finds a way opened up . . .
So ended this terrible thing.

The Bacchae

Characters

DIONYSUS, *the god of nature and wine, also called Bacchus, Evius, Bromius*

CHORUS, *women from Asia who have followed Dionysus as his devotees*

TIRESIAS, *the old and blind seer of Thebes*

CADMUS, *founder and former king of Thebes*

PENTHEUS, *grandson of Cadmus and king of Thebes*

A SOLDIER, *palace guard of Pentheus*

A HERDSMAN *from Mount Cithaeron*

AGAVE, *mother of Pentheus, daughter of Cadmus*

A MESSENGER, *a palace official*

GUARDS *of Pentheus*

WOMEN, *attendants of Agáve*

A SMALL CROWD *of Thebans*

Time and Setting

THE BACKGROUND: *It is the Heroic Age, many hundreds of years before the time of Euripides. Sémele, the daughter of Cadmus, during a love affair with Zeus had exacted from him the promise to grant her whatever she wished and was persuaded by the jealous goddess Hera (disguised as Sémele's nurse) to ask her lover to come to her as he came to Hera, in all his glory. Reluctantly Zeus complied. The mortal frame of Sémele could not support so much power, and she was consumed by lightning, giving birth in her death-stroke to a six months' child by Zeus, who then stitched the infant into his thigh and let him be born in due time as the god Dionysus.*

THE PRESENT: *It is some twenty years later. The action takes place on the acropolis of Thebes, outside the palace of Pentheus (in Doric style, with columns supporting an entablature). Nearby, fenced off by a trellis of luxuriant grapevines, is the tomb of Semele, from which a wisp of smoke still curls. The young king, Pentheus, new in his reign and apparently full of righteous intentions (though raw in self-knowledge), is determined to stamp out the worship of the young god Dionysus (his cousin), who has just returned to Greece from the East bringing with him the cult of the vine.*

Dionysus now enters stage right disguised as a man. He wears a panther skin loosely hanging from one shoulder, and a golden fillet binds his long, fair ringlets. In his hands he holds the sacred thyrsus,[1] a staff crowned with a rampant bunch of ivy. In spite of the

---

1. *Thyrsus:* usually a fennel stalk, with ivy inserted into or tied round the tip of its hollow stem. At a later date the ivy was sometimes twined round the stick, which was mounted with a green pine cone. The place of ivy in bacchic rites was perhaps older than the place of vine. Ivy was rent and chewed.

dreamy, even sweet expression of his eyes, he walks with a springy, lilting tread. On his lips plays an enigmatic, slightly ironic smile.

Prologue

DIONYSUS. So, the son of Zeus is back in Thebes:
I, Dionysus, son of Sémele—daughter of Cadmus—
who was struck from my mother in a lightning stroke.
    I am changed, of course: a god made man,
and now approach the rivulets of Dirce,
the waters of Ismenus.[2]   5
    [*bitterly*]
There by the palace is my mother's monument,
my poor mother, blasted in a bolt of light!
    Look, those ruins, her house, smoking still,
alive still with a most unnatural flame,
Hera's present to my mother . . .
it curls with undying insolence.

    But praised be Cadmus,
who made this untrodden ground,   10
this chapel to his daughter.
    And I, I have festooned it with green,
clustered it with vine.
    [*with a grand sweep*]
I come from Lydia,
its territories teeming with gold,
and from rich Phrygia.
    I am all-conqueror
in the sun-beaten steppes of Persia,
the walled cities of Bactria,   15
the wintry land of Media,
and in Arabia Felix—land of the blest.

    All Asia is mine,
and along the fringes of the sea
the pinnacled glory
of all those mingled cities
of Greeks and many races.
    But in this land of Hellas,[3]
this city Thebes
is the first place I have visited.   20
    Elsewhere, everywhere, I have established
my sacraments and dances:
to make my godhead manifest to man.

    Yes, here in Hellas, Thebes
is the first city that I fill
with the transports of ecstatic women.
    I've put their bodies into fawn skins,

2. The numbers refer to the Greek text, not the English.   3. *Hellas*: Greece.

thrust the aggressive thyrsus in their hands,   25
my ivied spear.
    You see, they should have known—known better—
they at least, my mother's sisters,
who said that I, Dionysus, was no son of Zeus;
that Semele simply loved a mortal
and then palmed off on the Almighty
(the idea was Cadmus's)   30
her unwed motherhood.
    "Don't we know," they cried,
"she lied about her lover, and that is why
great Zeus has struck her down!?"

    Aha! These sisters, these very same,
I've driven from their wits and from their homes:
    Out to the mountains and out of their minds.
    I've dressed them up as bacchanals
in my own orgiastic uniform;
and all the women of Thebes,
every female in this city,   35
I've started in a wild stampede from home
to join the Cadmus daughters.
    There they sit among the rocks,
under the silvery pines,
a congregation in the open.
    [*grimly*]
    Like it or not, this city has to learn
what it is to go through true conversion
to the rites of Bacchus.   40
    So, I defend my mother's cause,
making mortal man endorse
the fact I *am* a god
and born to her of Zeus.
    You know that Cadmus makes his grandson, Pentheus, king,
with all the kingly perquisites;
that Pentheus opens war on deity in me,
wards me off his sacrifice,   45
cuts me from his prayers . . .
    Very well,
I'll show myself to him and all of Thebes
a god indeed.
    And when everything has happened as I wish,
I'll remove myself to another land
and there reveal myself.   50

Should there be some trouble from the town of Thebes,
should they try to oust my maenads from the mountains,
I shall go out there myself
and lead my bacchants in the battle.

That is why I'm in this mortal form,
changed into the semblance of a human being.
> [*the sound of flute and timbrels and women chanting.*
> DIONYSUS, *suddenly alert, calls to them with enthusiasm*]

Onward!
My women of Tmolus,[4] you bulwark of Lydia,   55
my own sisterhood of worshippers;
whom I led out from foreign lands to be my company
in rest and march.
Raise up the native music of your home:
the timbrels[5] Great Mother Rhea[6] and I invented.
Surround the palace of Pentheus, the king.   60
Clash out the sound,
and turn this city out to see.
> [*looking away, stage right, toward the mountains*]

I hurry to the dells of Cíthaeron[7] where the bacchants are,
I go to join them in their dances there.
> [DIONYSUS *slips away as the* CHORUS *of oriental women
> moves into sight, chanting. They are led by a flute-player.
> Some of them have timbrels, some castanets*]

PARADOS OR ENTRY SONG

> [*in a vehement dithyrambic[8] hymn to* DIONYSUS, *the* CHORUS
> *celebrates his birth, his orgiastic rituals of music and dance
> on the mountains, and the enthusiasm of his devotees*]

FIRST VOICE. From the purlieus of Asia I come
Deserting Tmolus the holy   65
For the roaring god I toil
In an easy, exquisite task:
A paean to the praise of the god
Great Dionysus.
SECOND VOICE. Is anyone in the street?
Is anyone at home?
Let him go into holy retreat: 70
Silence on every lip
While I sing in the old, old way,
Glory to Bacchus.
THIRD VOICE. Happy the man whom the gods
Love, and whose secrets he knows—

4. *Tmolus*: a mountain in Asia Minor.
5. *Timbrels*: tambourines or kettledrums, the typical instruments in orgiastic cults.
6. *Great Mother Rhea*: a goddess of fertility.
7. *Cíthaeron*: a mountain in Boeotia sacred to Zeus and the Muses. Actáeon (see note to line 230) was torn to pieces by his own dogs here, and Heracles killed an immense lion on this mountain. And here, too, the baby Oedipus was exposed.

8. *Dithyrambic*: The dithyramb was a choral processional ode, harking back to the probable origins of Greek tragedy, in praise of Dionysus sometimes called Dithyrambus, "the twice-born," because after his birth he was stitched into the thigh of Zeus. This particular hymn—in dogma, myth, and ritual—seems to be based on an actual cult hymn, ancient even to Euripides.

Their rubrics—his life is designed
For sacred dances and joy:
In the mountains the wild delight   75
Of Bacchus in his soul,
His ritual he undergoes:
Cybele's orgies, great Mother's.[9]
He shakes the thyrsus on high.   80
With ivy he crowns his brow
For great Dionysus.

FOURTH VOICE. On, bacchanalians, on!
Bring Bromius[1] home, the god:
The son of the god—Dionysus—   85
From foreign Phrygian hills.
Bring Bacchus to the squares
The open squares of Hellas
Spacious for the dance.

FIFTH VOICE. Him whom his mother when gravid[2]
In bitter travail brought forth:
Him whom his mother miscarried
In a blast of light from Zeus,
He in that very chamber   90
Wherein her life was shattered
Was taken by Zeus and sheltered   95
Deep within his thigh:
Stitched with golden brackets,
Secreted from Hera.

SIXTH VOICE. He when the Fates had shaped him
A perfect baby there
His father then unfolded:
An ox-horned crescent god   100
Swaddled in the twisting
Serpents. That is why
The maenads[3] catch wild snakes and
Twist them in their hair.

SEVENTH VOICE. O Thebes, Sémele's nurse.   [*Strophe*] 105
  Put ivies round your turrets,
Break forth in green, O break
with bryony, its brilliant
Berries. Deck yourself
A bacchant with the branches
Of oak and fir. Put on   110
Skins of kid,[4] entassel
Your hems with silver fleece
Of goat. And with the fennel
Join reverence to riot.
Soon the land will dance;

---

9. *Cybele*: another name for Rhea, the fertility goddess.
1. *Bromius*: another name for Dionysus.
2. *Gravid*: pregnant.

3. *Maenads*: the bacchantes, or priestesses of Bacchus.
4. *Kid*: goat.

For whoso leads the revel
He is always Bacchus . . .   115
Will dance out to the mountains:
Mountains where the women
Waiting in their concourse
Rage from loom and shuttle
To rave with Bacchus.

EIGHTH VOICE. O Chamber of Curetes[5]   [*Antistrophe*] 120
You holy haunts of Crete
Who saw great Zeus' birthday,
In your caves the triple-
Crested corybantes[6]   125
Made the rounded timbrel
Tight with hide and beat its
Tense ecstatic jangle
Into the sweetened airs
Breathed by Phrygian-flutes.
They gave it in the hand of
Mother Rhea to drum-beat
Shouting bacchants raving.
The run-mad satyrs[7] snatched it,   130
Joined it to the dances
Biennially when Bacchus
In his feasts rejoices.

CHORUS OF VOICES. My love is in the mountains   [*Epode*] 135
Limp upon the ground he
Sinks: the revel races.
Vested in his fawn skin, he
Hunts the goat and kills it:
Ecstasy the raw
Flesh; and to the mountains
of Phrygia, of Lydia
He rushes: he is Bromius   140
    Evoë![8]
Leader of our dance.
The ground there flows with milk and
Flows with wine and flows with
Honey from the bees.
Fragrant as the Syrian
Frankincense, the pine fumes
From the torch our spellbound leader holds   145
High: its ruby flames

---

5. *Curetes*: Cretan spirits who saved the life of the infant Zeus by dancing and shouting so loud that his cries could not be heard. He had been hidden by Great Mother Rhea because Cronos, his father, had the habit of eating his newborn children.
6. *Corybantes*: male attendants of Cybele, also known for their revels.
7. *Satyrs*: woodland demigods who were part goat and part man. They were considered to be lust-driven creatures and were associated with Pan and Dionysus.
8. *Evoë!*: a cry used by worshippers either in praise or in supplication.

Flaring as he runs—
Shooting as he dances
    And while he cheers
His checkered followers forward
And shouts them to their feet
    His supple hair
Is rampant on the breezes.   150
    "Evoë!" he cries,
Loud among the maenads . . .
    "On my bacchants, on!
Chant to the glittering Tmolus
    With its golden streams;
    Chant to Dionysus,   155
Through the clash reverberant of tambourines.
    Cry down glory with your Phrygian cries
    Upon the god of joy.
    And all the while, the holy   160
    Honey-throated flute
    Holily invents
    Its piping gaiety
    For my roaring troubadours
    Raving to the mountains—   165
    Oh, to the mountains!"

Then the bacchanalian girl
Is full of happiness and gambols
    Lightfooted as a filly
Round its mother in the pastures.

First episode

[*enter* TIRESIAS, *the blind seer. He is dressed in a goatskin,
and his head is crowned with ivy. In spite of his age, his
manner is brisk, even excited. He knocks at the palace doors
with his ivy-crested staff*]

TIRESIAS. Where is the porter?   170
    [*a servant answers from inside*]
    Go, call Cadmus from the house—
that son of Agenor who came from Sidon
and raised the pinnacles of this Theban town.
    Will someone go and tell him Tiresias waits him.
    He knows already what we plan to do, he and I . . .
a man even older than I am, he he! . . . and yet   175
we dress the thyrsus up,
put our fawn skins on,
twine trailing ivies round our heads.
        [*enter* CADMUS, *also ancient and wearing a goat-skin. He is
        garlanded with ivy and supports himself on a luxuriant thyr-
        sus. Despite his age he is spryly gay, even impatient*]

CADMUS. Good! My intelligent old friend:
I knew it was you, even from the house,
the wise voice of intelligence.
 [they shake hands]
 I'm all ready, look:
complete in Dionysiac trappings.   180
 And why not?
He's my own daughter's child,
and he's proved his divinity to men.[9]
 So of course
we've got to work to build him up.
 [snapping his fingers and looking around]
Well, where do we dance?
Where do we let our footsteps fall
and waggle our decrepit grizzly heads?   185

Be my monitor, Tiresias,
one antique to another:
you the expert . . .
I'll never tire night or day
of drumming my thyrsus on the ground.
 [begins to thump his thyrsus on the flagstones]
Oh, how lovely to forget
just how old we are!
TIRESIAS. *[taking his arm]* My feelings too. I'm young again.
I too am going to try the dance.   190
 [they execute a rickety little jig together, but CADMUS *soon
 stops, panting]*
CADMUS. You don't think we should get a carriage
to take us to the mountain?
TIRESIAS. No, no: that wouldn't show the same respect
toward the god.
CADMUS. Well, shall one old man be nursemaid to another?
TIRESIAS. The god will show the way: we'll have no trouble.
CADMUS. Are we the only gentlemen in town to dance to Bacchus? 195
TIRESIAS. The only ones, all right; the rest all wrong.
CADMUS. Then we're wasting time. Here, take my hand.
TIRESIAS. Fine! Hand in hand . . . Yours in mine.
 [they totter forward for a few steps, then CADMUS *stops]*
CADMUS. I'm only a man. I don't belittle the divine.
TIRESIAS. No, *we* don't play at theologians with the gods. 200
We stay close to the hallowed tenets of our fathers:
as old as time.
 Nothing can undo them ever:
I don't care how brilliant or abstruse the reasons are.
 No doubt people'll say I've got no self-respect,
dancing, binding up my head with ivy—at *my* age . . . 205
 Well, then, let them.

9. A line sometimes rejected as an interpolation put in for greater clarity.

Where does the god assert
that only the young must dance—
or only the old?
He wishes to be worshipped by one and all,
not have his glory itemized.

CADMUS. [*watching the approach, stage right, of a resolute young
man*]
Tiresias—you can't see   210
so let me be your see-er,[1] ha!—
Pentheus is striding toward the palace,
you know, Echíon's son,
to whom I've given over the ruling of this land.
[*clicking his tongue*]
My, my, how upset he is!
What is he going to tell us now?

[PENTHEUS *enters. Shod in jackboots, wearing a short riding
tunic and carrying a hunting crop, he stalks into their presence with a brisk, no-nonsense manner. He is so full of what
he wants to say that he harangues the old men without at
first noticing their extraordinary fancy dress*]

PENTHEUS. I've come straight back from abroad   215
hurried home by rumors:
something very strange is happening in this town.

They tell me our womenfolk have left their homes—
in ecstasy, if you please—
go gadding to the mountains, the shady mountains,
dancing honor on this brash new god:
this—this Dionysus they've got hold of.   220

In the middle of each coterie of god-possessed
stands a bowl of wine—brimming.

Afterwards, they go sneaking off one by one
to various nooks
to lie down—with *men*;
giving out they're priestesses,
inspired, of course!
I warrant their devotion
is more to Aphrodite[2] than to Bacchus.   225

The ones I've rounded up,
my police have handcuffed
and safely slapped in jail.

The rest I mean to harry off the hills,
(including Ino and Agáve, my own mother,
and Autonóë, mother of Actáeon.)[3]   230

1. There is a play on words in the
Greek. Cadmus jests that on this occa-
sion he, and not Tiresias, is the seer.
2. *Aphrodite*: goddess of love, called
Venus by the Latins.
3. *Ino*: Ino and Agáve were Pentheus'
aunt and mother and were sisters. *Actáeon* was a cousin of Pentheus. Legend
has it that, one day while hunting, Actáeon saw Artemis (Latin name: *Diana*)
bathing naked in a woodland pool. This
chaste goddess was so angered that she
turned Actáeon into a stag, and he was
ripped to pieces by his own dogs. The
story has become the subject of numer-
ous paintings by the old masters, especially Titian. Another account of the
story is that Actáeon boasted of being a
better hunter than Artemis (who was
also the goddess of hunting), and that
was why she destroyed him (see lines
337–40). The lines within brackets are
thought by some to be an interpolation.

I'll capture them in iron traps—
put a stop to this immoral rollicking.
　　They say we have a visitor,
a mysterious wizard-conjurer from Lydia:
a fellow sporting scented goldilocks,   235
with rosy wine-flushed cheeks
and the spells of Aphrodite brimming in his eyes.
　　He passes nights and days with girls,
dangling in front of them his mysteries of joy.
　　Let me once catch him in this house—
I'll stop him tapping with his thyrsus,   240
tossing his mane of curls.
　　I'll separate his head from carcass.
　　This is the character who claims
that Bacchus is a god . . . Oh, yes, he does! . . .
stitched up once upon a time in Zeus's thigh.
　　Well, we know what happened to that little shoot:
sizzled by a thunderbolt along with mother and her lie—
she'd had the nerve to name   245
Zeus the Father as her lover.
　　What gall! What effrontery!
Enough to put a man in danger of the hideous noose . . .
Mysterious visitor, whoever he may be.
　　　　[*suddenly aware of the incongruous costumes of the two old
　　　　men*]
Ye gods! What is this?
Tiresias the prophet decked out like a spotted goat!
And my grandfather—it's preposterous—   250
playing the bacchant with a fennel wand?
　　Sir, sir, this is not my mother's father . . .
so ancient and so idiotic!
　　Please, throw away that ivy.
That thyrsus—get rid of it: let it go.
　　　　[*rounding on* TIRESIAS]   255
This is your idea, Tiresias:
another trick of yours to squeeze some profit
out of bird-watching and burnt offerings.
　　A new god, eh?
　　Introducing novelties to men?
　　Your gray hairs and nothing else
save you now from sitting down in chains
among these mad bacchants.
　　Ha! Bringing in such squalid rites . . .   260
　　When women get to celebrate with gleaming wine,
there's a ritual that's gone rotten. Oh, I'm telling you!
LEADER OF THE CHORUS. What blasphemy, strange man!
　　Have you no reverence for the gods?
　　No reverence for Cadmus,
who sowed the famous crop of dragon's teeth?
　　Is Echíon's son to bring his family to disgrace?   265
TIRESIAS. [*turning to* PENTHEUS] A clever man with an honest brie͡f
finds it easy to be fluent.

Your tongue, sir, runs on glibly
as if you really made some sense,
but in fact you're talking nonsense.
A brash bold man
who lets himself depend entirely on his tongue   270
is a dangerous citizen—and a foolish one.
This new god you think so fatuous,
words cannot encompass
the greatness of his coming power in Hellas.
I tell you, young sir,
mankind has two blessings:
Deméter[4] is the one, the goddess,   275
(Earth, that is—call her what you will),
who keeps men alive with solid food;
the other is Sémele's son,
who came afterward and matched her food with wine.
He it was who turned the grape
into a flowing draft
and proffered it to mortals
So when they fill themselves with liquid vine
they put an end to grief.   280
It gives them sleep
which drowns the sadness of each day.
There is no anodyne for sorrow.
[Therefore when we pour libations out][5]
It is the god himself
we pour out to the gods,
and so, do men some good.   285
You ridicule the myth
of his being stitched inside the thigh of Zeus.
Let me teach you how you should interpret that.
When Zeus had snatched the baby god
from the searing fork of light
and sheltered him on Mount Olympus,
Hera wanted him expelled from heaven;
but Zeus thought up a scheme to counter this—
as one might imagine from a god.
He chipped off a piece of sky that domes the earth
and presented it to nagging Hera
as a disembodied dummy Dionysus.[6]   293
In time, however, men confused the word
and said the child had been *embodied* into Zeus
instead of being just a substitute to humor Hera—
a god's sop to a goddess.
And so the story was invented
of his being sewn up inside a godhead's thigh.   295

---

4. *Deméter*: goddess of the harvest and grain (Latin name: *Ceres*). Paired with Dionysus, she represents bread, he wine.
5. This line is not in the Greek but is so strongly implied in the text that it is difficult to leave out.

6. It is possible only to paraphrase lines 293–95. A crucial line (or lines) is missing; and there is, moreover, no equivalent English for the play on words on which the exegesis turns.

He is a god of prophecies.
Those whom his spirit fills become possessed
and have clairvoyant powers;
and when he takes a person absolutely, 300
he mouths the future through that person's mouth.
He also has assumed some of Ares' duties.
A regiment in arms, for instance,
actually in line of battle,
has been known to bolt in all directions
without a spear being raised.
This hysteria too is something sent by Bacchus. 305
A day will come when you shall see him
on the very rocks of Delphi,
plunging over the pronged peaks of Parnassus
with his pinewood torches flaring,
shaking his bacchic thyrsus—
tossing it in the air.
All through Greece his name shall be extolled.
So, listen to me, Pentheus:
Do not imagine men are molded by sheer force, 310
or mistake your sick conceits for insights.
Welcome this god to Thebes.
Pour out libations: yes,
wreathe your head and revel in his mysteries.
It's not for Dionysus to make women modest. 315
Foolproof chastity depends on character.
and in the corybantic celebrations
no decent woman is seduced.
　　[he points to a small crowd that has gathered]
Look, even you are gratified
when a crowd stands at your gates 320
and the name of Pentheus is exalted in the city.
It is not improbable, I think,
that he also would like to be acclaimed.
I therefore, Sire, and Cadmus, whom you ridicule,
shall wreath ourselves with ivy and shall dance:
an ancient grizzly couple, it is true,
but dance we must;
and no argument of yours
shall ever make me spar with gods. 325
　　[turning as if to go]
You are a fanatic, sir. A sick fanatic.
There is no cure for madness
when the cure itself is mad.
LEADER. *[fervently]* Your argument, old man,
does no dishonor to Apollo[7].
and yet most shrewdly treats
Bromius as a mighty god.

---

7. *Apollo*: god of the sun and of proph-　mous shrine was at Delphi.
ecy, among other things. His most fa-

CADMUS. [*in his best conciliatory manner*]
   My boy, Tiresias has advised you well.   330
      Stay with us.
      Don't break with our old ways.
      You are all in the air just now.
      Your reasons are unreasonable.
      Even were this god no god, as you insist,
   tell yourself he *is*:
   act out a very advantageous lie,
   which makes our Sémele, just think of it,
   the mother of a god.   335
      The whole family can take credit.
       [*dropping his voice*]
      You know the miserable mistake Actáeon[8] made:
   how those meat-eating dogs of his
   (which he had reared himself)
   tore him piecemeal in these very dells.
      All because he bragged
   he was a better huntsman than   340
   the goddess Artemis.
      Do not risk the same.
       [*places an arm on* PENTHEUS' *shoulder*]
      Come, let me put some ivy round your head.
      Be one with us in honoring the god.
PENTHEUS. [*pulling away*] Keep your hands off.
      Go and play at bacchanals.
      I don't want your foolishness wiped off on me.
      Your feeble-minded preacher
   will reap what he deserves.   345
       [*turns savagely to the crowd and points to* TIRESIAS]
      Go, someone, on the double:
   get to this man's lair
   where he scrutinizes birds.
      Heave it up with crowbars,
   turn it upside down;
   make a shambles of the place.
      Throw his holy ribands to the winds,   350
   yes, to the whirlwinds:
   that'll touch him on the raw—more than anything.
       [*striding about*]
      Others of you go and scour the realm.
      Track this foreign effeminate down
   who infects our women with a new disease,
   befouls our beds.
      If you catch him, bring him here in irons.   355
      I'll have him stoned—
   the death that he deserves.
      He'll find his fun in Thebes

---

8. *Actáeon*: see note to lines 62 and 229–30. The reference in line 337 clearly is an example of dramatic irony forshadowing Pentheus' fate.

not so very funny.
 [*exits, sweeping into the palace*]
TIRESIAS. [*gazing in his direction and slowly shaking his head*]
 Poor fool! You don't know what you say.
 You were out of your mind before.
 Now you rave.
  [*to* CADMUS *in a small voice from which all enthusiasm has
  been drained*]
 Cadmus, let us go—you and I—   360
to beg the god in spite of this man's boorishness
to be merciful to him and merciful to Thebes.
  [*extending a hand*]
 Come with me and bring your ivy staff.
 You'll help to hold me up, as I will you.
 It would be embarrassing
for two old men to fall . . . but so be it—   365
the god Dionysus must be served.
 Oh, Cadmus, yes, you must make sure
that Pentheus, that sorry man,
does not swamp your house with sorrows.
 This is not a prophecy but sober fact:
foolhardy says as foolhardy does.
  [*the two old men hobble away together*]

FIRST CHORAL ODE

 [*echoing the fears of* TIRESIAS, *the* CHORUS *sings an ode to
 the Spirit of Holiness, which does not turn its back on the
 sacraments of Bacchus and the simple acceptance of the
 things that bring love, peace and happiness to men*]

Holiness, angel of heaven   [*Strophe 1*]370
Holiness gliding on golden
Wings over earth, do you hear
 This man's unholy
Impudent mocking of Bacchus,   375
Sémele's son, the primal
god of gladness and garlands
among the blessed immortals.
Whose reign is the trance, is the dance,
With flute and with laughter;   380
Is cessation from cares at the feasts of the gods
When the bloom of the grape and the crater of wine
 Throw sleep (in the shadows)   385
  Round ivy-crowned men.

The braggart's unbridled tongue, [*Antistrophe 1*]
The anarchical folly of fools
Leads to untimely demise.
But the life of the quietly wise,   390
 Unshaken abides,
Holding the home together.

For the gods in the faraway skies
  Still look upon men.
Mere cleverness is not wise.   395
Life, given immortal airs,
  Shortens and dies.
And a man in pursuit of mere grand desires
Misses his time. Oh, that is the way   400
  Of fanatically, willfully mad
    Men, I surmise.

Oh, to set foot on Cyprus,   [*Strophe* 2]
  Island of Aphrodite!
Where the Spirits of Love, the Erotes,
Stroke us with magic—poor mortals;   405
Or the strange and myriad-mouthing
  Deltas of Paphos
Which load it with fruits without rain;
Or where, flush in her beauty, Pierîa
  Is seat of the Muses;   410
Or the holy hill of Olympus . . .
There, there, Bromius, lead me
  In romp and in reverence;
  For there dwell the Graces,
  There is Desire   415
And there it is holy
To revel with Bacchus,

[PENTHEUS *has re-entered from the palace and stands listening*]

The divine son of Zeus, who rejoices   [*Antistrophe* 2]
  In blossomy feasts and abundance:
  Lover of Peace, great Irenë
  who cherishes young men and bliss.   420
He gives to the rich and he gives to the poor
  His wine, sweet spell against sorrow;
  Despiser of him who despises
Living his days and loving his nights   425
Content to the end, or wise in his keeping
Mind and heart from passing beyond
          The horizons of man . . .   430
          Whatever the many,
          The simple, allow—
          that will I follow.

Second Episode

[*a group of* SOLDIERS *enters from outside the city—audience's right—bringing in* DIONYSUS *as the Mysterious Stranger. He is manacled and pinned by the arm*]

SOLDIER. [*laconically*] King Pentheus, all present and correct, sir.

We've made the catch you sent us to.   435
The operation was successful.
> [*prods the prisoner forward, but not ungently*]
The animal we found was tame, sir:
put himself without resistance in our hands;
didn't even blanch
or lose that wine-rose glow of his;
actually smiled and said we'd *got* to handcuff him . . .
even waited for me,
to make my job the easier.   440
    I felt quite awkward, and I said:
"Sorry, sir, I have no wish to take you in,
but that's King's orders, sir."
    Meanwhile, if you please,
those raving women that you rounded up and manacled
and clapped into the public jail—
they're free, they've vanished,
gone gamboling off to the mountain glens,   445
shouting out the name of Bromius, their god.
    The fetters on their feet just fell apart,
the prison doors slid back their bolts—
and not a human touch.
    He's chock-full of miracles, sir, this man,
this stranger visiting our Thebes . . .   450
the rest is up to you.
PENTHEUS. Take his handcuffs off.
    He is in my trap.
    No agility will set him free.
> [*the* SOLDIER *unfastens his hands.* PENTHEUS *looks him up and down with distaste*]
Hm, my man—not a bad figure, eh?
At least for the ladies:
which is why you came to Thebes.
    Nice curls too . . .
no good for wrestling, though.   455
    Very fetching, all the same:
the way they ripple round your cheeks.
> [*walking round* DIONYSUS *as if he were buying a slave*]
And such clear skin!
You take good care of it—
keep it out of the sun, what? . . .
hunt Aphrodite and beauty in the shade.
> [*wheeling round on him*]
Well, who are you?
Where do you come from, first?   460
DIONYSUS. [*smiling*] Without boasting I can easily tell you that.
Have you heard of Tmolus, the mountain of flowers?
PENTHEUS. Certainly. It ranges in a ring round Sardis city:
DIONYSUS. I am from there. Lydia is my country.
PENTHEUS. What makes you bring these rituals here to Greece?

DIONYSUS. Dionysus sent me: the son of Zeus.   465
PENTHEUS. Some Zeus! Does he breed new gods there?
DIONYSUS. [*still smiling*] No, the same Zeus there wedded your own Sémele here.
PENTHEUS. Did he overwhelm you in a dream? Or with your eyes wide open?
DIONYSUS. Face to face . . . He gave the rituals of possession.   470
PENTHEUS. Rituals of possession? Of what peculiar form?
DIONYSUS. They may not be divulged to the incommunicate.
PENTHEUS. Well, what do the holy communicants gain by it?
DIONYSUS. [*his smile growing subtle*] You may not hear . . . But it would be good to know.
PENTHEUS. Clever of you, what? You make me want to hear.   475
DIONYSUS. The god's rites do not welcome a curious, impious man.
PENTHEUS. [*slyly*] You say you clearly saw the god. What's he like?
DIONYSUS. That is up to him, not something I arrange.
PENTHEUS. Another neat evasion. It tells me nothing.
DIONYSUS. To the foolish ear the wise speak foolishly.   480
PENTHEUS. Is this the first place, then, you've brought your god?
DIONYSUS. By no means: every land in Asia celebrates his dance.
PENTHEUS. Naturally! Foreigners have much less sense than Greeks.
DIONYSUS. In this they have much more. Traditions differ.
PENTHEUS. And these celebrations that you make—
are they at night or day?   485
DIONYSUS. Mostly at night. There's mystery in the dark.
PENTHEUS. Of course! It's perfect for seduction, for undermining women.
DIONYSUS. Some can dig out dirt even in broad day.
PENTHEUS. Licentious sophistry! You ought to be rewarded.
DIONYSUS. And you for crass impieties against the god.   490
PENTHEUS. Ho ho! Our mystery priest gets bold:
an acrobat with words!
DIONYSUS. Tell me my sentence, then: the worst that you can do.
PENTHEUS. First I'll—I'll chop your dainty love-locks off.
DIONYSUS. [*still smiling*] My hair is holy. I grow it for the god.
PENTHEUS. Next, hand over that—that decorated staff.   495
DIIONYSUS. Try to take it from me. I carry it for Bacchus.
PENTHEUS. I'll shut your carcass up—oh, safe in prison.
DIONYSUS. And when I wish, the god himself will set me free.
PENTHEUS. Indeed? When you stand among your bacchants, begging?
DIONYSUS. He is beside me now and sees my trials.   500
PENTHEUS. Really! Where? My eyes cannot see a thing.
DIONYSUS. Where I am . . . But you, blasphemer, cannot see.
PENTHEUS. [*to the* GUARDS] Seize him. He's laughing up his sleeve at me and Thebes.
DIONYSUS. Hands off, I say! You'll be sorry if you bind me.
PENTHEUS. And I say bind him. I am in command.   505
DIONYSUS. [*looking straight through him*] You—you do not know

what your life is, what you do, or even what you are.

PENTHEUS. [*shaken in spite of himself*]
I—I am Pentheus, Agáve's son:
Echíon is my father.

DIONYSUS. [*the smile has become sinister*]
Pentheus, yes: the name spells sorrow.
It fits you perfectly.

PENTHEUS. Away with him: lock him in the stables near.
Give him all his darkness and his murk.   510
[*turns viciously on the* CHORUS]
And these women that you brought with you,
These associates in your evil work,
I'll either have them sold
Or give their fingers something else to do
Besides just thumping drums and beating tympanums.
I'll keep them slaving at my looms.

DIONYSUS. [*solemnly calm*] I shall go,
But nothing not my destiny can come on me.   515
And Dionysus, whom you say does not exist,
Will wreak revenge on you for this.
When *I* am the one that you molest
It is *he* that you arrest.
[*the* GUARDS, *followed by* PENTHEUS, *lead* DIONYSUS *away.
Then the* SOLDIERS *close in upon the* CHORUS]

SECOND CHORAL ODE

[*in a desperate appeal to Thebes, the* CHORUS *denounce
their persecutor and call on their god*]

O daughter of Achelóüs   [*Strophe*]
O Dirce,[1] holy maiden: 520
Once in the well of your waters
You welcomed the baby of Zeus,
Who sired him and snatched him
Out of the living embers
And into his thigh ensconced him,
Shouting: "Dithyrambus,[2]   525
In this male womb of mine
Be buried and be famous
With his name in Thebes:"
      Yes, O Bacchus!
Then why, beatific Dirce,   530
When I come to you in garlands
Do you spurn my spellbound dances
And thrust me from your kingdom?
Why do you scorn and flee me?

1. *Dirce*: a stream in Thebes named after a river nymph. Apparently she had been a worshipper of Dionysus and had been transformed into a stream as a reward for giving the infant Dionysus sanctuary.
2. *Dithyrambus*: Dionysus.

The grapes of Bacchus one day,   535
Full of grace—believe me—
  Will make you love him.

Infamous Pentheus proves his[3]   [*Antistrophe*]
Earth-bound line, his birthday
From dragon and from snake-man.   540
A freak and a monster he,
No normal human being:
A butchering earth-born giant
In war with the divine.
He'll manacle me soon   545
Dionysiac though I am.
He holds in his house already
Deep in his murky keep
My leader in the dance-spell.

Do you see these things, O son of   550
Zeus, O Dionysus?
Your votaries on trial
Grappling with oppression.
Descend, Lord, from Olympus:
Shake your golden thyrsus.
Quell this man of blood's
  Brash obsession.   555

Where on Nysa, nurse of fauna,   [*Epode*]
Are you, Dionysus, leading
Wild processions with your thyrsus?
Up among Corýcia's crags?[4]
On Olympus deep in green   560
Bowers where the harp of Orpheus
Making music marched the trees
Toward him once and marched the savage
Beasts . . . Oh, blessed are you, valley
Of P¡ería: Bacchus loves you.   565
He will come and set you dancing
With the rubrics of possession.
He will cross the racing river
Axius, lead his maenads whirling   570
Through the streams of Lydias, father
Of all currents: he who fathers
Wealth and well-being for the world,
Letting loose his lovely waters
Through a land made rich for horses.   575

[the SOLDIERS, *who have been listening* [*impressed in spite
of themselves with the devotion of the* CHORUS] *now at a*

---

3. I follow Bothe and Hermann (and Professor Dodds's inclination) in omitting
line 537 as an interpolation: δταν δταν
ὀργὰν ("What, what flaming rage!").

See Euripides, *The Bacchae*, ed. E. R.
Dodds (Oxford: Clarendon Press, 1966).
4. *Corýcia's crags*: Corýcia was a nymph
associated with Mount Parnassus.

word of command break ranks and begin to hustle the
women away. *Suddenly, there is a crack of thunder, the
earth quakes, buildings rock, and lightning plays over the
tomb of Sémele. The soldiers scatter, the women run about
shrieking, and the voice of* DIONYSUS *rings from the heart of
the palace*]

Third Episode

CHORAL DIALOGUE

DIONYSUS. Hó! Hulló![5]
D'you heár me cálling—heár my voíce?
Hulló, bacchanálians! Hó, bacchántes!
CHORUS. Whát is it? Whát is it? Whére is the voíce
Cóming from, cálling me stráight from Bácchus?
DIONYSUS. [*clear and louder*] Hulló, hulló! Heár me agaín: 580
Són of Sémele, són of Zeús.
CHORUS. Máster, our máster! Hó, hulló!
Cóme to our cómpany, cóme to dánce
Hólily, Brómius, Brómius, hó!
[*more tremors and a clap of thunder*]
DIONYSUS. Térrible Énnosis[6]—
Spírit of eárthquake—sháke the eárth.   585
[*the architrave of the palace cracks*]
CHORUS. Áh, aáh!
The cástle of Péntheus shívers and soón
sháll be sháken to rúin.
FIRST VOICE. Gréat Dionýsus is ín the pálace:
Bów down befóre him.
SECOND VOICE. Bów we dó.   590
Lóok at the cápitals cráck from the píllars.
Brómius is chánting in the wálls.
DIONYSUS. Tóuch off the thúnderbolt's sízzle of líght.
Búrn down, O búrn the pálace of Péntheus.   595
[*lightning sears through the buildings and bursts a new
flame from Semele's ever-smoldering tomb*]
CHORUS. Aah! Aah!
Look, d'you see the fire leaping
Round Sémele's holy tomb?
The very fire the god of thunder
Left there once: the bolt of Zeus.
[*masonry crashes down and the* CHORUS *throw themselves
on their faces*]
Down on the ground, fling yourselves bodily,   600
Terrified maenads . . . Look, our master

---

5. *Hó! Hulló!*: cries of supplication or
praise used in worship.
6. *Ennosis*: Poseidon, or earthshaker

(Latin name: *Neptune*), brother of Zeus
and Hades.

Is turning the palace upside down:
  The son of Zeus.
    [*the doors burst open and* DIONYSUS, *still in disguise but
    wreathed in smoke and smiling, stands brandishing his
    thyrsus.*]
DIONYSUS. [*playfully*] Come, my oriental ladies[7]—
  Have I frightened you so well
  You have fallen to the floor?
  It seems you did not miss how Bacchus   605
  Shook and shivered Pentheus' palace.
  Come, get up and stop your trembling.
    [*the* CHORUS *pick themselves up and gaze with relief and
    admiration at* DIONYSUS]
LEADER. O brightest light of bacchic dancing,
  Sweet it is to see you safely.
  Alone we were and quite abandoned.
DIONYSUS. Did you lose all hope when Pentheus   610
  Plunged me into gloomy prison?
LEADER. Yes, of course, for who could guard us
  When yourself had met with trouble?
  How ever did you flee the clutches
  Of that man who has no conscience?
DIONYSUS. Liberated by myself!
  I did it with the greatest ease.
LEADER. Were your hands in handcuffs? Weren't they   615
  Locked by him in manacles?
    [DIONYSUS *steps among the* CHORUS *amused and pleased*]
DIONYSUS. Ha! there I made him look so foolish:
  For when he thought that he was binding
  Me he did not even touch me.
  He was gorged on pure delusion.
    [*the women form a ring around him*]
  In the stables where he shut me,
  There he came across a bull:
  Began to throw his slipknots round it,
  Bind it by the hooves and knees,
  Panting with emotion, dripping   620
  Sweat in drops from off his body,
  Digging teeth into his lips while
  I sat by and quietly watched him.
  Bacchus came and shook the building,
  Fired the tomb of Sémele.
  Pentheus saw it, thought the palace
  Was on fire: ran about
  Ordering slaves to carry water: 625
  Every slave was put to work
  All for nothing. When he thought

---

7. I have followed Euripides in going into trochees, lines 604–40.

I'd escaped, he stopped his labors,
Charged into the palace, lunging
With his dark and gloom-drawn sword.
Meanwhile Bromius (or I thought so—
I can only give a guess)
Made a phantom Pentheus flew at   630
in the courtyard, stabbing only
Thin, bright air, but fondly thinking
He was really butchering *me*.
   [*laughing to himself*]
Bacchus had much worse in store:
Flattened out the stable buildings,
Turned the whole thing into rubble.
Ha! How Pentheus must regret his
Putting me in prison!
               Sheer
Exhaustion now has made him drop his
Sword. He's prostrate . . . Not surprising,   635
Seeing a man has challenged a god.
As for me, I calmly walked
Out of the house—here to you—
Without a second thought for Pentheus.
   [*turning his head*]
Ah! It sounds as if his jackboots
Stamp along the hall: Milord will
Show himself.
            What will he say
After this?
Let him come out snorting tempests,   640
I shall be the soul of peace.
A cool detachment is the thing
For a man of wisdom—eh?
   [DIONYSUS, *with a wink at the* CHORUS, *leans easily on his
   thyrsus and directs a dreamy, somewhat supercilious gaze
   toward the palace doors, where the stamp of the king's boots
   reaches its climax and* PENTHEUS *bursts out of the palace*]
PENTHEUS. It's a disgrace: the stranger's got away,
  bound up as he was just now in chains.
   [*sees* DIONYSUS *and gasps*]
  Awh! . . . The man is here . . . what?   645
  However did you manage to get out . . .
  to materialize outside my door?
DIONYSUS. Keep your feet and keep your anger quiet.
PENTHEUS. How did you shed your chains and get out here?
DIONYSUS. Did I not say—or did you not listen—
  that somebody would set me free?
PENTHEUS. Who? . . .
With you it's one queer saying on another.   650
DIONYSUS. He who grows the clustering grape for man.

blessing

PENTHEUS.[8] Ho, Dionysus! . . . A pretty benison *he* gave to man!
It ought to make him blush.
DIONYSUS. [He came to Thebes with nothing but good things.]
PENTHEUS. [*turning to his* SOLDIERS]
Ring round the town . . . Seal off every outlet. That's an order.
DIONYSUS. Whatever for?
Can gods not somersault your walls?
PENTHEUS. Clever, very clever, but not quite clever enough!   655
DIONYSUS. Supremely clever—in what is necessary.
[*he breaks off with an expectant look toward the country,
from which a* HERDSMAN *is now seen approaching*]
However, listen first to what this man
has come to tell you from the mountains.
[*nodding to the* CHORUS *and smiling*]
We shall wait for you. We shall not run away.
[*the* HERDSMAN *is dressed in homespun, with a tasseled cap,
a smock over cloth breeches, and goatskin tied round his feet
for footwear. One may assume—though perhaps it is not
necessary—that he was among the crowd which gathered
outside the palace earlier and heard* PENTHEUS' *speech of
scorn*]
HERDSMAN. [*with excitement and awe*]
O Pentheus, ruler of this realm,   660
I come here straight from Cíthaeron.
Where the dazzling snowdrifts never leave the ground . . .
PENTHEUS. [*cutting him short*] Yes, You've come straight here to
tell me what?
HERDSMAN. Oh, sir, I've seen the raving ladies:
those who streamed out from their homes stung mad,   665
their white limbs flashing.[9]
I am bursting to tell you, King, and tell the town
the terrible things they do, past all wondering.
But first, sir, may I know
if you are really ready to hear what's going on,
or must I trim my tongue?
Your quick temper frightens me . . .   670
your hot temper. sir—too much like a king.
PENTHEUS. Speak on.
From me you do not have a thing to fear.
It is never right to fume at honest men.
But the more appalling your account
of these intoxicated worshippers,
the more appalling my recriminations   675
on that crooked man who undermined these women.

8. There is a line (or lines) missing between 652 and 653. I am swayed by Professor Dodds's inclination to give this
line to Pentheus and the missing line or
lines to Dionysus. See the full note
about the problem in Dodds, p. 158. The
conjectural line is here supplied by
Dodds from Wecklein: καλῶν μὲν οὖν
τη᾽δ᾽ἦλθε τὴν πόλιν πλέως.
9. λευκόν κῶλον: often translated as
"barefoot." The bacchantes usually were,
but Euripides does not actually say this.

HERDSMAN. Our pasturing herds had just begun to climb
　the uplands at the hour the sun's first rays
　break their warmth upon the ground,
　when I see three bands of women who have danced:　　　680
　Autonóë at the head of one,
　Agáve your own mother, of the second,
　and Ino, so, the third:
　all stretched out in sleep.
　collapsed at random
　wherever they had tossed:
　Some lying on their backs upon the piney needles,
　others pillowed on the oak-leaved floor—　　　685
　all modestly, not as you suggested, sir:
　not in their cups, or in a flute-enducéd trance,
　or any wild-wood chase of love.
　　Then, your mother, at the lowing of the horny cattle,
　stood up in the middle of the bacchic ones
　and called upon them loudly to bestir their limbs from sleep.　　690
　　And they shook the rank sleep from their eyes
　and straightened up . . .
　　　[*pausing with wonder*]
　　A sight most strangely orderly and beautiful:
　women young and old, and maidens still unmarried.
　　First they let their hair fall down their shoulders,　　695
　then fastened up the fawn skins that were loose,
　and girdled snakes with licking jaws[1]
　around their dappled hides.
　　Some fondled young gazelles
　or untamed wolf-cubs in their arms
　and fed them with their own white milk:　　700
　those, that is, who were young mothers
　with babies left at home
　and breasts that burgeoned.
　　Then they wreathed their heads
　with ivy, oak, and bryony in flower.
　　One of them took up her thyrsus,
　struck the rock,
　and water gushed from it as fresh as dew.　　705
　　Another hit her rod of fennel on the ground,
　and the god for her burst forth a fount of wine.
　　Anyone who fancied liquid white to drink
　just scratched the soil with fingertips
　and had herself a jet of milk;　　710
　while from their ivy-crested rods
　sweet streams of honey dropped.
　　Oh, if you'd been there, sir, and had seen,

1. Euripides' phrase λιχμῶσιν γένυν
("licking the cheek") is often translated
as meaning the women's cheeks. I do
not think this is what he means. It
would be difficult for snakes as girdles
to achieve this. I believe he intends the
snakes' flickering, forked tongues.

you would have come with prayers
toward the god whom now you execrate.
    We cowherds and shepherds came together,
talked among ourselves, debated
these marvelous goings-on.   715
And then a fellow who was fond of gadding up to town,
very glib of speech,
held forth to all of us and said:
    "Hey, you people here,
who live upon these holy mountain terraces,
what d'you say we go and hunt Agáve out,
Pentheus' mother,
chase her from her mad ecstatic rapture   720
and do a service to the king?"
    He spoke convincingly, we thought,
so we laid an ambush in the copses
and hid ourselves.
    At a certain hour
the maenads shook the thyrsus for the bacchic dance
and with a common throat called out:
    "Iacchus,[2] son of Zeus, great Bromius!"   725
    Then the whole mountainside
became convulsed and god-possessed,
even the animals:
nothing but it moved with the mystic run.
    Agáve, as it happened,
came sprinting past me
and I leapt out to seize her
from the ambush where we hid.   730
    But she, at the top of her lungs, cried out:
    "Come, my flying hounds,
we are being hunted by these men.
Wield your thyrsus in defense
and follow, follow after."
    Well, we fled:
escaped being torn to pieces
by these god-struck maniacs   735
who with their naked hands fell upon our heifers
grazing on the grass.
    You could see a woman with a bellowing calf
actually in her grip,
tearing it apart.
    Others ripped young cows in little pieces.
    You could see their ribs and cloven hooves   740
being tossed up high and low;
and blood-smeared members dangling from the pines;
greatly lordly bulls,
one minute glaring

2. *Iacchus*: Dionysus.

in all the pride of their horns,
the next dragged to the ground like carcasses
by the swarming hands of girls,   745
and the meat flensed from their bodies
quicker than you could wink a royal eye.
        They burst like a wave of birds over the ground,
skimming across the flat fertile delta lands
of the river Asopus (so rich for Thebes).   750
        They tore like an invading army
into the villages of Hýsiac and Erýthrae,
which nestle on the lower spurs of Cíthaeron,
and turned them upside down.
        They snatched up babies out of homes.
        The loot they loaded on their shoulders   755
stayed put without being tied.
        Nothing tumbled to the ground,
not even brass or iron.[3]
        They carried fire on their flowing heads,
and it did not burn them.
        The villagers,
enraged, of course, at being plundered,
took arms against these manic ones.
        Then, what a spectacle, my King, how sinister!   760
        Their spear points drew no blood,
while the women, hurling thyrsi from their hands,
oh, the women wounded men, set men to flight . . .
that was not without some unknown power.
        They went back then
to the place where they began,   765
to the fountains which the god had sprung for them.
        They washed their hands of blood
and from their faces the serpents licked the clotted gore.
        After all this, my lord,
whoever this spirit be,
you must receive him in our city.
        He is powerful in many things.   770
        He even—so I'm told—gave wine,
that sorrow-curing cup, to human beings.
        Sir, if the god of wine does not exist,
then neither does the goddess of love:
no pleasures left for man.
LEADER. I hesitate to speak my mind before the king   775
        but cannot keep from saying:
        there is no greater god than Dionysus.
PENTHEUS. So,
        like a wildfire it already hurries here,

3. Something is probably missing after line 756 in the Greek. Professor Dodds suggests the herdsman may have continued with: "Nothing resisted their as- sault, not bolted doors, not bronze, not iron." It is not likely that the maenads would have wanted to carry away pots and pans.

outrageously, this mass hysteria:
disgracing us before the whole of Thebes.
    [*wheels round to the captain of the* GUARDS]
    There's not a moment to be lost.
    Go the the Electran Gate,[4]   780
call out the heavy infantry,
and the mobile cavalry in full,
all—all who can bear a shield or spring a bow:
we must march against the mad bacchants.
    It is not to be endured
    It goes too far . . .
if we let these women get away with this.   785
DIONYSUS. [*gravely*] So you are not moved, Pentheus,
    by any words of mine!
    Nevertheless,
in spite of all you've done to me,
I cannot help but tell you:
you must not take up arms against a god.
    Rather, be still:
Bromius will never let you hustle his possessed   790
from their ecstatic hills.
PENTHEUS. No sermons, if you please.
    You have broken out of jail: savor that . . .
    or I shall have the law on you again.
DIONYSUS. Would you so? If I were you,
    I'd offer offerings up to him
    and not offense.   *cattle herding*
        Don't kick against the goad: *prod*
    a man against a god.   795
PENTHEUS. Offerings? Yes, indeed,
    a most appropriate sacrifice:
    women's blood and massacre
    in the glens of Cíthaeron.
DIONYSUS. [*quietly*] You will be routed—all.
    And what a disgrace:
    the bacchanaliann thyrsus
    beating back your shields of bronze!
PENTHEUS. [*strutting toward his* GUARDS]
    Can't get the better of our stranger—can we?   800
    Passive or active, he has the answer!
DIONYSUS. Friend, it is still possible to mend these things.
PENTHEUS. By doing what?
    Making myself my own subjects' slave?
DIONYSUS. I shall bring the women here
    wielding no weapons.
PENTHEUS. Exactly—another trick of yours.   805
DIONYSUS. Trick? It is my sole device to save you.

---

4. *Electran Gate*: one of the seven gates of Thebes.

PENTHEUS. No, it is a conspiracy with them
to make your bacchic rituals permanent.

DIONYSUS. Conspiracy, if you like—that much is true!
but with a god.

PENTHEUS. [*turning to leave*] Servants, bring my armor here.
And you, stop talking.

DIONYSUS. [*with a new and sinister light in his eyes*] Wait!   810
How would you like to see their mountain séances?

PENTHEUS. [*slowly turning around*] Very much.
I'd pay a fortune in gold for *that*.

DIONYSUS. Why? What gives you such a strong desire?

PENTHEUS. [*hedging*] Well . . . of course . . .
I should be sorry to see them drunk, but . . .

DIONYSUS. But, you would like to see them—sorrow and all?   815

PENTHEUS. To be sure, if I could crouch quietly under the pines.

DIONYSUS. They would discover you, though you came unseen.

PENTHEUS. Then, openly . . . I take your point.

DIONYSUS. [*smiling*] Well, shall we go? You'll undertake the journey?

PENTHEUS. [*the words slipping out*]
Yes, yes! I can hardly wait to start.   820

DIONYSUS. Then you must put on a linen shift.

PENTHEUS. What! I, a man, be taken for a woman?

DIONYSUS. They'll kill you if they see you as a man.

PENTHEUS. You've made your point again . . . always a wise one,
what?

DIONYSUS. [*still smiling*] Dionysus here advises me.   825

PENTHEUS. [*nervously*] But how shall I carry out what you suggest?

DIONYSUS. I shall go inside and dress you up myself.

PENTHEUS. What kind of dress—a female's? I shall look a fool.

DIONYSUS. [*pretending to turn away*]
So you are no longer anxious to watch the raving maenads?

PENTHEUS. What is this dress you say I have to wear?   830

DIONYSUS. I'll fit you with a wig of spreading locks.

PENTHEUS. [*gulping*] And . . . and the next item in my outfit?

DIONYSUS. A thyrsus in your hand, and a spotted fawnskin on.   835

PENTHEUS. [*turning on his heel*] No, no, I can't . . .
cannot bring myself to dress up as a woman.

DIONYSUS. [*grimly*] Then you'll have to battle with the Bacchae
and spill blood.

PENTHEUS. [*stalling*] All right, then. Let us go and watch them first.

DIONYSUS. That's better: more sensible than hunting viciousness
with vice.

PENTHEUS. But how shall I pass unseen through the Cadmean
capital?   840

DIONYSUS. We shall go an unfrequented way, and I shall lead.

PENTHEUS. Yes, yes, anything,
so long as I'm not jeered at by the bacchic women.
[*weakly*]
Come, let us go inside and . . . and there I must decide.

DIONYSUS. As you please.
I am ready for all contingencies.

PENTHEUS. [*with a show of independence*] So, I shall go in, then: 845
either to set out for the mountains armed or . . .
or fall in with your plans.

> [PENTHEUS *walks into the palace.* DIONYSUS *follows but
> turns at the doors toward the* CHORUS *with an eerie, menac-
> ing smile*]

DIONYSUS. The fish, my women, heads now for the net.
He will reach the Bacchae, punishment, and death.
So, Dionysus, to your work.
You are not far.
Let us be revenged on him.
Make his mind unsteady first: 850
Imbue him with a dizzy fantasy.
Sane, he never will consent
To put a woman's clothing on;
But, once deranged, he will.
I want the whole of Thebes to laugh
(after all his threats and arrogance)
As he walks, a woman, through the town.   855

> [*he moves toward the doors*]

Now to go and groom him in the gown
He shall wear to Hades and his death:
Pentheus, murdered in his mother's grasp,
Will come to know full well
Dionysus, son of Zeus—
a real god at last: 860
To man most gentle
And most dangerous.

> [DIONYSUS *goes swiftly into the palace*]

THIRD CHORAL ODE

> [*a passionate song of hope. Heaven is not mocked. Happi-
> ness is a thing of the spirit, very different from greedy pride
> or mere success. To find the true daemon within you and to
> pay him homage is the real bliss*]

O tell me, shall I   [*Strophe*]
Ever again
Dance in a spell through the night
With the flash of my white
Feet, and my head thrown back in the clean   865
Dewy air, like a fawn at play in the green
Joy of a meadow, escaped
From the flight of the chase when she leapt
Clear of the mesh of the net

And the ring of the eyes that watched;
When the hallooing huntsman braced
    His hounds for the race,   870
And over the water-flat fields she fled
    Tense as the breeze
To solitudes empty of men,   875
    Oh, to the sweet
Shooting green underneath
The shadowy hair of the trees?

    What is wisdom? What is fairer   [Refrain]
    Heaven-blest in sight of man,
    Than to hold a hated rival's
        Head beneath one's hand?   880
    What is fair is dear forever.

Slowly but surely divine   [Antistrophe]
    Power begins
To move into action and fell
The brutally minded man:
He who in wild delusion refuses   885
To worship the gods . . . But the gods creep up
    By stealth in the creeping of time
On the irreligious man.   890
To know or to meddle beyond
The divinely established norm
    Is utterly wrong.
    Slight is the price
Of an act of faith in the numinous strength   895
Of what has been grounded in being:
Believed in as long as time.

    What is wisdom? What is fairer,   [Refrain]
    Heaven-blest in sight of man,
    Than to hold a hated rival's   900
        Head beneath one's hand?
    What is fair is dear forever.

Lucky the sailor who flees   [Epode]
    From storm into port.
Lucky the man who rides
    Above all his cares,
In one way one or another   905
Surpasses in riches and power.
There are always a thousand hopes
For a thousand mortals, and some
Hopes are crowned with success;
Others run into sand.
To me the one who is lucky
Is he who day by day lives happy.   910

Fourth Episode

[DIONYSUS *enters from the palace. His demeanor has changed. The latent power which underlay his smiling meekness has broken surface and shows him in a new and ruthless light. He no longer tempts but commands. Now he summons* PENTHEUS *from the palace in a voice that rings with a cruel authority*]

DIONYSUS. Come on out, you perverted man,
  so passionate for what is not for sight
  and acts that are not right—
  out, Pentheus, I say, before the palace.
    Show me what you look like
  dressed up as a woman—
  a mad woman and a maenad—   915
  prying on your mother and her mob.
    [PENTHEUS *enters, shuffling, from the palace. He is clearly altered. In terms of modern breakdown techniques we should say he shows every symptom of having been brainwashed.* "What follows DIONYSUS on *the stage is less than man: it is a giggling, leering creature, more helpless than a child, nastier than an idiot, yet a creature filled with the Dionysiac sense of power and capable of perceiving the god in his true shape, because the god has entered into his victim.*"[5] PENTHEUS *is now dressed as a maenad, with a wig of long, flowing hair, a band round his head, a linen shift pleated like a priest's alb reaching his feet, and in his hands the ivy-crowned thyrsus*]

DIONYSUS. [*derisively*] My word! You do look like one of the
  Cadmus daughters.

PENTHEUS. [*peering*] Yes, yes: I'd say I see two suns,
  a double city Thebes,
  twin sets of seven gates,
  and a bull seems to beckon me—   920
  He walks before me.
    [*leaning toward* DIONYSUS *with his mouth open*]
  Now I'd say your head was horned . . .
  or were you an animal all the while?
    For certainly you've changed—
oh, into a bull."[6]

DIONYSUS. [*as if talking to a child*]
  The god is walking with us: before unfriendly,

---

5. Dodds, p. 192.
6. Euripides' line is: ἀλλ' ἦσθα θήρ; τετάυρωσαι γάρ ὀυν. Professor Dodds comments: "The dragging rhythm . . . due to the strong pause of the third foot, suggests the King's slow bewildered utterance" (Dodds, p. 193, note 920-22). I make a similar break. It is possible that Pentheus sees another figure behind the Stranger: his double, but with horns— Dionysus in his beast incarnation. A sinister effect could be had by the use of two actors, one bull-headed, one speaking the more ominous lines.

but he's made his peace with us, and now
you see things as you ought.

PENTHEUS. [*preening himself*] Well, how do I look?
Don't I have Aunt Ino's carriage absolutely?   925

DIONYSUS. [*winking at the* CHORUS]
Seeing you, I'd say my eyes saw *them*.
[*walks round, surveying him*]
Tut tut! A curl is out of place—
not as I fixed it underneath your riband.

PENTHEUS. [*guiltily*] It must have shaken loose inside the house   930
when I was tossing my head, being a bacchanal.

DIONYSUS. [*stepping up to him*]
Let me put it into place again. I'm your lady's maid.
Now hold your head up.

PENTHEUS. There, *you* dress it, please. I'm all yours now.

DIONYSUS. [*scolding*] Tch! Tch! Your girdle's loose.   935
And your skirt's all uneven at the ankles.

PENTHEUS. [*solemnly looking down at his toes and then twisting
round to see the back*] Yeah I think so too: especially on the
right foot.
On the left heel, though, it's hanging well.

DIONYSUS. [*fiddling with the clothing*] You're going to call me
your best friend, I think,
when you see the bacchants, to your surprise, stone sober.   940

PENTHEUS. [*not listening*]
Do I hold the thyrsus in the right hand or the left
to make myself a better bacchanal?

DIONYSUS. Hold it in the right: lift it in strict time
to the right foot . . . I'm so pleased
your mind is changed.

PENTHEUS. [*with an upsurge of magical strength*] Do you think I
could lift the whole of Cithaeron,
bacchants and all, high upon my shoulders?   945

DIONYSUS. You could that—if you wished.
You were not healthy in mind before.
Now you are—exactly right.

PENTHEUS. Shall we take up crowbars?
Or should I put an arm and shoulder to the crags
and tear the peaks up with bare hands?   950

DIONYSUS. Come now, no destroying the purlieus of the nymphs:
the places where our Pan[7] sits piping.

PENTHEUS. Yes, you are right.
Moreover, women are not won by force . . .
I'll hide myself among the pines.

DIONYSUS. Ah! The hiding place to hide you in you'll find   955

---

7. *Pan*: The god of shepherds and of
huntsmen, he was a monster in appear-
ance. He had two horns on his head, his
complexion was ruddy, and he was a
goat from the waist down. He is said to
have invented the flute. He resided
chiefly in the rugged hillsides of Arcadia.

when we've crept up on the maenads for your peeping.
PENTHEUS. [*leering*] I fancy I can see them in the bushes now;
all couched down like little birds in love-nests.
DIONYSUS. That's exactly what you're going to watch.
Perhaps you'll take them by surprise . . .   960
if *you* are not taken first.
PENTHEUS. [*thrusting out his bosom*] Conduct me through the
public heart of Thebes:
the only man of them that has the courage.
DIONYSUS. [*with a sly glance at the* CHORUS]
The only man that . . . lets himself be vulnerable
for this city, yes, the only one.
And so the struggles that await you must be yours.
Come then, I shall take you safely there . . .
another bring you home.   965
PENTHEUS. Oh, yes, my mother.
DIONYSUS. A sight for all to see.
PENTHEUS. [*Coyly*] You talk of pampering me.
DIONYSUS. In your mother's arms.
PENTHEUS. [*giggling*] You're trying to spoil me now!
DIONYSUS. In a very special way.
PENTHEUS. And yet I merit it.   970
[*he begins to walk*]
DIONYSUS. [*laughing behind* PENTHEUS' *back*]
Oh, you are formidable
And what you walk toward
Is formidable indeed.
You will find a fame
That hoists you to the skies.
[*with sinister enthusiasm as* PENTHEUS *disappears*]
Open your arms, Agáve,
And you her sisters: daughters
Of Cadmus. This young man
I lead out to a fine
Contest wherein I
and Bromius shall conquer.   975
The rest shall soon be seen.
[*exit* DIONYSUS]

FOURTH CHORAL ODE

[*a hymn of vengeance, covering the interval during which
the events unfolded later are actually taking place, now clair-
voyantly seen by the* CHORUS. *Knowledge is not more real
than mystery, nor the unconscious mind less than the
conscious*]
Hurry, you hounds of hell, to the mountains where [*Strophe*]
The daughters of Cadmus hold their wild séance.
    Worry them into a frantic trance
Against the man disguised in the dress of a woman: 980

A roaring one who comes to spy on the maenads.
Oh, as he peers from the rump of a rock or top of a tree-trunk
     His mother will see him first.
Then she will call her spellbound band: "Hulloo!
Who is this searcher that comes—has come—to the
     mountains   985
     And pries on us Cadmean daughters:
We who run to the hills, the hills, to revel, O Bacchus?
     Who was it that bore him?
     He's not of the blood of a woman
     But whelpéd from a she-lion
     Or some Libyan Gorgon.[8]   990

     Let Justice visible walk   [*Refrain*]
     Let Justice sworded walk
     To strike through the throat and kill
This godless, lawless ruthless man: 995
     This earth-sported scion
     Spawned from Echíon.

How he lawlessly, ruthlessly, raving advances   [*Antistrophe*]
On you and your mother's god-possessed worship, O Bacchus!
     Expecting his lunatic cunning   1000
     And cheating courage to master by force
What cannot be conquered. For such aberrations death
Is the discipline—yea, yea—divine dispensation requires
     The homage of man for a life
To be lived without sorrows. Oh, cleverness never was mine.
I am ready to hunt it down.   1005
These others, these loftier things, are simple and lead
To a beautiful life, yes, pure and pious as long as the day
     And into the night
     It sheds from it everything wrong   1010
     In pursuit of the right
     And homage to heaven.

     Let Justice visible walk   [*Refrain*]
     Let Justice sworded walk
     To strike through the throat and kill
This godless, lawless, ruthless man
     This earth-sported scion   1015
     Spawned from Echíon.

     Appear as a bull, or be seen as   [*Epode*]
           a many-headed dragon.
     Or come as a fire-breathing
           vision of a líon,
     Yes, Bacchus, come and snare him,

8. *Libyan Gorgon*: one of the Gorgons, three monstrous sisters who had snakes on their heads instead of hair. They were so horrible that it was said if a mortal looked upon one of them he would turn to stone. After Perseus slew Medusa and was flying over the Libyan desert with her severed head, the drops of blood that fell on the sand turned into serpents, which have infested the area ever since.

this hunter of the bacchants   1020
With a smile on your face enmesh him
            under the deadly netting
Of maenads' mad stampeding."

Fifth Episode

[*a messenger, the personal attendant of* PENTHEUS, *staggers in from the country. He is breathless and disheveled*]

MESSENGER. Ah . . . house once happy . . . throughout Hellas!
    House of that old man of Sidon   1025
who harvested the dragon's seed in the reptile's land . . .
    how I weep for you—
    slave though I am.[9]
LEADER. Why, what is it?
    Have you news of the bacchic ones?
MESSENGER. Pentheus is no more—Echíon's son.   1030
LEADER. [*in a cry of triumph*] Lord Bromius, your godhead is
    made manifest.
MESSENGER. What was that? Woman, do you mean to say
    my master's end can give you joy?
LEADER. I am an alien and shout in foreign tunes.
    I am no longer hunched in fear of fetters.   1035
MESSENGER. But do you reckon Thebes so poor in men that . . .
LEADER. It is Dionysus, ah, not Thebes!
    that holds dominion over me.
MESSENGER. That I understand . . . But is it seemly, ladies,
    to crow upon a down-and-out disaster?   1040
LEADER. Tell it all, explain exactly, how he died,
    this perverse man—this purveyor of perversion.
MESSENGER. [*moving into the center*] When we had left behind
    the homesteads of our Theban countryside,
and crossed the waters of the Ásopus,
    we struck into the foothills of Mount Cíthaeron,   1045
Pentheus and I (for I attended on my master),
together with that stranger who was acting as our guide.
    After we had settled in a grassy clearing,
our feet and tongues as quiet as we could—
    to see and not be seen—   1050
there in a glen cliff-bound and full of streams
we saw them—yes, the maenads—
sitting in the crowded shadows of the pines,
their hands all busy with their happy tasks.
    Some were making thyrsi thick again   1055
with crests of ivy tresses;
some, frolicsome as fillies loosed from festal yokes,
chanted back and forth in Dionysiac antiphons.

9. I omit line 1028 as an interpolation,   See Dodds, p. 206, note 1027–28.
"Good slaves suffer with their masters."

Pentheus, unhappy man,
could not see this throng of women, saying:
"Stranger, from where we stand
I cannot quite make out these spurious maenads,   1060
but if I climbed a tall pine on the precipice
I should have a perfect view of them
and all their perpetrations."
　　Then I saw the stranger do a marvelous thing.
he slowly let the pine-trunk spring up straight,
began to bend it downward—down and down
toward the dark earth, till it arched there like a bow   1065
or like a peg-line compass curving
the circumference of a wheel.
　　So the stranger took that mountain pine,
took it in his hands and tugged it to the ground:
a feat beyond a mortal human being.
　　Then, lodging Pentheus on this tip of pine,   1070
he slowly let the pine-trunk spring up straight,
carefully slipping it along his grip,
not to throw him off again.
　　Sheer into the sheer sky it went,
my master sitting straddled on the top:
much plainer to the maenads now than they to him.   1075
　　Scarcely had he settled into sight
high up on this perch
than nowhere was the stranger to be seen
and a voice from somewhere in the ether came,
calling:
　　"My maidens, look, I bring you
the man who made a mock of you and me,   1080
our rituals of possession:
see you punish him."
　　And while the voice yet spoke
there streaked from heaven to earth a flame,
an uncanny flare of light.
　　The very air stood still
and in the glens the woods themselves
held stillness in their leaves,
and from the beasts no cry was heard.   1085
　　But the bacchants had not caught the voice distinctly,
and, leaping to their feet, they gazed around.
　　Then the voice exhorted them a second time,
and when the daughters of Cadmus recognized
the clear behest of Bacchus,
they shot forth like ringdoves on the wing,   1090
such was their speed of stride:
Agáve, his own mother, and her sisters
and all the bacchanals.
　　Up the valley, through the torrents,

over boulders, there they leapt,
breathing out the very spirit of the god.

    And when they saw my master perched upon the pine,   1095
first they tried to climb up near him on a pinnacle
and, using all their might, to pelt him down with stones.

    Some threw shafts of pine branch at him,
others sent their thyrsi flying through the air
in a miserable attempt to reach him.   1100

    But still their aim fell short
of the poor fated wretch,
trapped and sitting there past all escape—
the distance far outdid
even their fanaticism.

    At last,
like a stroke of lightning,
they stripped an oak tree of its branches,
and, using them as levers,
tried to pry the tree up from its roots.

    When all these efforts were of no avail,   1105
Agáve said:
"Come, my maenads, make a circle round the bole
and grip it fast.

    We must take this climbing animal
or he will spread abroad the secrets
of our god-struck dance."

    A rage of hands then swarmed upon the pine
and loosened it from earth.   1110

    Then, down,
down from his high perch towards the ground,
plunged Pentheus
with one continuous yell,
aware of what was going to come.

    His mother
as the priestess of the bloodbath
was the first to fall upon him.

    He snatched the headband off his hair[1]   1115
to let Agáve, wretched woman, see
who it was and so not murder him.

    He touched her on the cheek and cried:
"Mother, it is I, your child, your Pentheus,
born to you in Echíon's house.
Have mercy on me, Mother,   1120
and because of my mistakes
do not kill your son—your son."

    She was foaming at the mouth.
    Her dilated eyeballs rolled.
    Her mind was gone—
possessed by Bacchus—she could not hear her son.

---

1. presumably to take his wig off.

Gripping his left hand and forearm   1125
and balancing her foot against the doomed man's ribs,
she dragged his arm off at the shoulder . . .
it was not her stength that did it
but the god's power seething in her hands.
   Ino, active on the other side,
was ripping at his flesh;
and Autonoë now and the whole rabid pack were on him.   1130
   There was a single, universal howl:
the moans of Pentheus (so long as he had breath)
mixed with their impassioned yells.
   One woman carried off an arm,
another a foot, boot and all;
they shredded his ribs—clawed them clean.
   Not a finger but it dripped with crimson   1135
as they tossed the flesh of Pentheus like a ball.

His body lies in pieces:
some of it under the gaunt rocks,
some of it in the deep green thickets of the woods—
by no means easy to recover . . .
except for his poor head,
which his mother, seizing in her hands,   1140
has planted on the thyrsus point.
   She fancies it the head of a mountain lion
and carries it through the heart of Cíthaeron,
leaving her sisters still capering with the mad ones.
   She is on her way here inside these walls,   1145
exulting in her most pathetic quarry;
raising up her voice to Bacchus
as her "master of the hounds,"
her "master of the hunt" . . .

What a prize champion!
What a tear-drenched triumph!
   But I am going: I mean to get away
from this most grisly happening
before Agáve reaches home.
         [*turns to the* CHORUS *with a dead stare, answering their pre-
         vious question (line 877) in a passionless voice*]
That is fairest which is humble   1150
Obeisance to heaven.
That is also wisest wisdom,
So I think, if men could follow.
         [*exit* MESSENGER]
         [*the women sing of triumph, but as their thoughts turn
         from* PENTHEUS *to* AGAVE, *the song becomes tinged with pity
         and horrific irony*]
Dance away now for great Dionysus

Sing away, sing for the doom that befell
The dragon's descendant, Pen-the-us: 1155
Who dressed himself up in the dress of a woman
   And, blest with the fennel
   Wand (for his dying),
Was led by a bull to his wild
Demise. O, Cadmean bacchants
What infamous paean have you   1160
Fashioned of sorrow and crying!
   How pretty a triumph
   To plunge red hands
Into the life of one's child!

LEADER. Look, I see surging towards the palace   1165
   the rolling-eyed Agáve, Pentheus' mother.
   [*a swell of chanting and cries*]
   Welcome to these happy myrmidons
of the happy, shouting deity!
   [*enter* AGAVE *with her troupe of maenads. The lyric dialogue
   which follows marks a climax of horror.* AGAVE, *in a grisly
   pas seul, with her bloodied clothes, her voice and eyes wild,
   and the head of* PENTHEUS *mounted on her thyrsus, dances
   with the* CHORUS *while the rest of her maenads form a ring
   around them, clapping and miming*]

AGAVE. [*thrusting the head toward the* CHORUS]
   Bácchants from Ásia, loók!

CHORUS. [*recoiling*] No!
   Múst you exhórt me? óh!

AGAVE. [*pointing to the top of her thyrsus where the hair of a
   human head takes the place of ivy*]
   Sée what we bríng you dówn
      from the móuntains hére to these hálls: 1170
      a béautiful cútting. Óh,
      such wónderful húnting!

CHORUS. I sée it. I sée it . . .
   Jóin in our dáncing.

AGAVE. [*stroking the matted hair*] Withóut a tráp I trápped him:
   this ténderest whélp of a térrible lión.
      Lóok, don't you sée it?   1175

CHORUS. From whére in the wílderness? Whére?

AGAVE. Cíthaeron.

CHORUS.   Cíthaeron?

AGAVE.   Cíthaeron bútchered him.

CHORUS. Whích of you smóte him?

AGAVE. Í was fírst to. Í won the príze.
      Lucky Agáve, they cáll me   1180
      in our bácchic seánce.

CHORUS. Nóbody élse?

AGAVE.   Yes, Cádmus's . . .

CHORUS.   Cádmus?

AGAVE. Cádmus's dáughters
    hándled this créature áfter
    Í did; but ónly áfter . . .
    Óh what a béautiful húnt!²

Cóme, jóin in the feást.   [*Antistrophe*]
CHORUS. [*drawing back in horror*]
    The féast? . . . Aáh, poor wóman!
AGAVE. [*gently pulling her fingers through his beard*]
    How lóvely and yóung, little búll!   1085
    Your chéek is júst growing dówn
    únder your délicate crówn.
CHORUS. [*humoring her*]
    He loóks like a béast of the wíld with his háir.
AGAVE. Yes, Bácchus, that cléverest húntsman
    místered the máenads agaínst him   1190
    in súch a cléver deplóy
CHORUS. Of coúrse: our kíng is a húnter.
AGAVE. Do you práise me?
CHORUS. We práise you.
AGAVE.   And sóon
    Cádmus's sóns . . .
CHORUS. [*testing her delusion*]
    Togéther with Péntheus, *yóur* son . . .   1195
AGAVE. Will práise his móther for cátching
    this cúb of a líon.
CHORUS. It's lárger . . .
AGAVE.   Oh, lárger!
CHORUS.   Much lárger than lífe . . .
    Só, you are háppy?
AGAVE. In ráptures
    for the kílling, the glóry,
    of my móst remárkable húnt.
    [*end of lyric dialogue*]
LEADER. [*very sadly and softly*]
    Then hold up—you poor, unhappy woman—   1200
    this hunting trophy that you've carried home,
    for the whole of Thebes to see.
AGAVE. [*proudly mounting the palace steps and holding out* PEN-
    THEUS' *head*]
    Come, all of you who live
    in this lovely town and realm of Thebes:
    come and see the quarry,
    the animal, we Cadmus daughters
    have caught and killed . . .
    and not with nets or thonged Thessalian spears,   1205
    but with our own hands—our own white arms.
    Oh, why must huntsmen brag,

---

2. Here two lines (Chorus?) are probably missing.

who go and get their useless tools from armorers,
when we with our own bare hands took *him*
and ripped apart our animal
joint by joint?   1210
> [*turning to a slave*]
> Where is that old man, my father?
> Let him come out here.
> And Pentheus, my son, where is he?
> Let him fetch a ladder,
> set it up against the house
> and nail this lion's head
> high on the facade:
> this lion I went hunting, I,
> and have brought home.   1215
> [*the* SLAVE *comes back leading* CADMUS *from the palace.
> Behind them, other* SLAVES *carry a bier on which are the
> remains of* PENTHEUS *covered with a sheet.* CADMUS, *still in
> his bacchanalian gear, an exhausted, hopeless old man, turns
> to the bier-carriers*]

CADMUS. Come, follow me with your forlorn load.
> Follow me, servants, carry him home:
poor Pentheus, whose dead remains
in a dismal search I found
scattered in a thousand pieces
through the glens of Cíthaeron,
deep in the woods,
undetectable,
not one fragment together with another.   1220
> [*he pauses to control himself*]
> I had left the bacchants and come home
and was already in the city walls
with old Tiresias,
when someone told me of my daughters' perpetrations.
> I turned back at once,
back to the mountain,   1225
to redeem this son left lying by the maenads.
> There I saw Autonóë
(she who once bore Aristaéus his Actaéon)
and Ino also:
both among the oak woods still,
still flushed with their ghastly frenzy.
> But Agáve, with frenetic pace, someone told me,
was on her way here   1230
> [*suddenly sees her and shudders*]
> So it is true—I see her:
a far from blessed sight.

AGAVE. [*preening and parading herself*]
> Father, you can make the grandest boast:
you've sired the finest daughters in the world—
oh, by far!—

All three of us, I say, but me especially.   1235
I've deserted loom and shuttle
and gone on to greater things:
to wild beast hunting with bare hands.
    [*she carefully takes the head from the thyrsus, cradles it in
    her arms, and offers it to Cadmus*]
In these arms, as you can see,
I carry the prize I won:
hang it in your halls.
    [CADMUS *steps back*]
Receive it, father, in your hands.   1240
Celebrate my hunting prowess.
Call in your friends and feast.
You are a lucky man:
lucky because of me and what I've done.

CADMUS. [*with averted head*] Oh, immeasurable distress!
    Vision beyond all seeing:
    Murder
    Is what your tragic hands have done.   1245
    Beautiful the victim
    Cut down by the gods:
    The sacrificial feast
    You call me to and Thebes.
    I weep for your misfortune—
    Yours and then for mine.
    How just but overwhelming
    The god who brings us down:
    Bromius, our master,
    Though begotten of our line.   1250

AGAVE. [*turning to her group with a grimace*]
    How disagreeable old age is . . . in men!
    How crabbed of eye!
    I wish my son took after *me*:
were a great hunter,
went hunting wild animals with the other youths of Thebes.
    Hm, he is only good, that fellow,
for picking quarrels with the gods.   1255
    [*naggingly*]
He ought to be corrected, father,
and you're the one to do it.
    Well, is no one going to call him here
before my eyes, to witness my success?

CADMUS. [*with a groan from the depths*]
    Oh, if you ever come to understand
what it is you've done,
you'll suffer with a suffering past belief.   1260
    But if until the end,
you stay forever in the state you are,
this misery will be some miserable relief.

AGAVE. Ha! What is there amiss in this?

What call for sorrow?

CADMUS. [*gently taking her arm*] Turn your eyes, first please,
to the skies up there.

AGAVE. I am looking.
And what am I supposed to see?   1265

CADMUS. Is it still the same—
or do you see some change?

AGAVE. [*Dreamily*] It is lighter than before:
more luminous.

CADMUS. And do you feel the same . . .
the same unrest inside your soul?

AGAVE. I do not understand your meaning . . .
[*with a slight twinge*]
I seem to be becoming . . . somehow . . . aware.
Something in my mind is . . . changing.   1270

CADMUS. Can you hear me?
Can you answer me distinctly?

AGAVE. [*from a long way away as if waking up*]
Yes . . . but I've forgotten . .
What were we talking of, my father?

CADMUS. Whose house did you marry into, child?

AGAVE. You gave me to Echíon:
sprung from the dragon's teeth, they say.

CADMUS. And in your house—
the son you gave your husband,   1275
who was he?

AGAVE. Pentheus—the son we had together.

CADMUS. Then—
whose face is this
you are holding in your hands?

AGAVE. It is a lion's . . . or,
they that hunted it said so.

CADMUS. [*gripping her hand*] Now look straight at it.
It does not cost you much to look.

AGAVE. [*turning and staring*] Aah! What am I seeing?
What am I cradling in my arms?   ·   1280

CADMUS. Gaze at it: study it more clearly.

AGAVE. O–h!
I see a giant grief:
myself in agony.

CADMUS. [*remorselessly*] Does it look to you just like a lion?

AGAVE. No . . . No . . . It is Pentheus' head I hold—
wretched . . . fatal woman!

CADMUS. Yes, *I* keened[3] for him   1285
long before you even knew.

AGAVE. [*scarcely audible*] Who murdered him?
Who put him in my hands?

CADMUS. Ah, ruthless truth, how unseasonable you are!

3. *Keened*: mourned audibly.

AGAVE. Tell it:
  break my heart with horror
  of what is still to come.
CADMUS. You killed him, you
  and those sisters that you have.
AGAVE. [*in a drained voice*] Where . . . was it done?   1290
  At home or somewhere . . . else?
CADMUS. Where once before
  dogs tore Actáeon apart.
AGAVE. [*with a gasp*] Cíthaeron?
  What evil genius possessed him to go there?
CADMUS. He went to mock the god
  and you at your bacchic rites.
AGAVE. But we, however did *we* get there?
CADMUS. Out of your minds.
  The whole city was possessed by Bacchus.   1295
AGAVE. [*under her breath*] Destroyed . . . by Dionysus . . .
  now I understand.
CADMUS. You bristled with rank hubris:
  you denied his deity.
AGAVE. [*her tears streaming onto* PENTHEUS' *head*]
  My son's dear body, Father? Where is that?
CADMUS. Here. We are carrying it, so arduously retrieved.
AGAVE. Are the limbs all put together—decently composed?[4]   1300
    [CADMUS *gives a silent nod toward the bier*]
AGAVE. But how did Pentheus share my madness?
CADMUS. He proved himself to be like you,
  a blasphemer of the god;
  and so the god has brought us down together
  all in a single crash:
  you, your sisters, Pentheus, and me,
  to obliterate my house—
  for I have no son . . . no,   1305
  now that I see
  this sapling from your womb—
  you stricken woman—
  most hideously and horribly cut down.
    [*turns his gaze to the bier*]
  Light of this house's eyes,
  son, my grandson,
  pillar of my palace beams!
    This city held you in its awe;   1310
  and as for this old man,
  no one while *you* were near had a wish to slight me,
  for you would make him pay for it in full.
    But now,
  I shall be sent home, disgraced:
  I, Cadmus the great,

---

4. After this line, there is a gap in the manuscript of at least three lines.

who sowed the Theban race
and harvested a crop so beautiful.   1315
   O dearest Grandson,
even dead, I count you with the dearest still;
but never will you touch this beard of mine again,
or call me Grandfather, hug me, son, and say:
"Is anyone annoying you?   1320
Is anyone a nuisance, rude, upsetting you?
   Tell me, Grandfather . . .
I shall punish every single man who does you wrong."
   But now,
I am bereft and *you* are lost,
your mother racked, our family broken.
   Does any man dismiss the powers above?   1325
Let him gaze on this poor creature's end
and acknowledge the divine.

LEADER. I feel your pain, poor Cadmus,
for though your grandson reaps
no less than he deserves,
the pain is yours.

AGAVE. [*falling on her knees*] Father you see,
how everything for me is overturned . . .⁵

AGAVE. Everything is deserted, dark . . .
and who but myself put out the light?
   O brutal hands, burning with gore,
yesterday you washed and sped
this baby to his bed
and now you wash yourselves in a stripling's blood!
   Wicked hands, that waited
till the hour was rich with royal promise,
you should have decked a young man for his bride
and now you dress his corpse
to speed him to the world below.
   [*turning to* CADMUS]
See, Father, these polluted fingers
already pale and rinsed with tears—

5. There follows a gap of about fifty lines in the manuscript. They include Agáve's lament and the farewell of her son, and the first part of Dionysus' speech. From various external sources and from a couple of mutilated fragments, we can form a general picture of the contents of the lacuna. I paraphrase them here as Professor Dodds lists them in his useful note on line 1329 p. 234.

Agáve, flung in a moment from ecstasy to despair, and conscious of being a polluted creature, begs permission to lay out the body for burial, and to bid it a last farewell. Cadmus consents, warning her of the conditions.

Over the body she accuses herself and moves the audience to pity, embracing each limb in turn and lamenting over it. Dionysus now appears above the castle, and first addresses all present, speaking of the Theban people who denied his divine origin and rejected his gift, and of the outrages for which Pentheus has paid with his life. He then predicts the future of the survivors, each in turn. The Cadmeans will one day be expelled from their city: they have themselves to blame for it. Agáve and her sisters must at once leave Thebes for ever; it is a sacrilege for murderers to stay in the city. Finally, the god turns to Cadmus, whose fate survives in the manuscript almost complete. Between lines 1329 and 1330 I have inserted a dramatic reconstruction of the missing Greek.

they beg to make amends . . .
   Grant me this at least,
to touch each limb and bid farewell
to the body of my son.
CADMUS. So be it, Daughter.
   Prepare his poor remains
to fit his journey to the dead—
but with dispatch:
a filicidal killer
may not linger on the harm she did.
AGAVE. [*kneeling by the bier*] My son, my son,
whom these blind fingers tore apart
and these callous eyes attacked,
we know not what we do
when we pride ourselves we know.
   [*she kisses and touches each member in turn*]
   This head
of matted curls
once nestled on my breast.
   These arms
that held a scepter for a day
lie lifeless by these mangled flanks.
   These young legs
that should have run exulting in the chase
are racked and blood-torn.
   [*turning to the* CHORUS]
   Pity me, you women,
I who must compose from ruins
the noble edifice
she so lately has demolished.
   Fetch some princely shroud
that we may caparison for burial
the body of a king.

FIFTH CHORAL ODE

Great Dionysus, breaker of barriers,   [*Strophe*]
   Son of the Father imperial:
Vine-clad god and priest of the natural,
   Sodden with light in purpureal
Cypress glooms and mystical pines,
   Now we adore and address you.
Capture the nights and ambush the days
   Of the impiously stupidly clever,

And those that depend on the march of the brain   [*Antistrophe*]
   And the force of the master plan
To alter the wages of man, and think
   To know better. O Bacchus, evoë!

Bind us with bryony, ivy, and everything
  Round us and under us, over us,
And let every peak of Cíthaeron ring
  With the triumph of animal holiness.

EXODUS OR DENOUEMENT

DIONYSUS. You shall be changed into a snake.[6]   1
  And your wife, Ares' daughter,
whom you married though you were a mortal,
shall take reptilian shape as well.
  You shall drive a chariot drawn by bullocks
with your consort at your side
(so says Zeus's oracle)
leading a barbarian tribe.
  Their uncountable battalions
shall ransack many cities;   1?
but when they loot Apollo's shrine
they shall receive short shrift on their return.
  You, however, and your wife,
Ares shall preserve,
translating you to the land of the blessed ones
and everlasting life.

> [*the women of the* CHORUS *begin, amost imperceptibly, t
> sway, playing gently on flute and tambourine.* DIONYSU
> *continues*]

This, I speak to you—
  as no mortal man
    but Zeus-begotten.   13<
If only you had been
  willing to be wise,
    instead of otherwise,
You would be happy now:
  your friend, the son of Zeus.

CADMUS. [*tottering forward and holding out his hands*]
Have mercy, Dionysus
  we have sinned.

DIONYSUS. Too late to know me now:
  you did not when you should.   134

CADMUS. Ah! . . . We understand,
  but you are merciless.

DIONYSUS. And all because you flouted
  my born divinity.

CADMUS. But gods should not repeat

---

6. "This bizarre prediction has puzzled mythologists no less than it startles the common reader. The story bears traces of having been put together at a relatively late date out of heterogeneous older elements." Thus Professor Dodds, who gives a detailed exegesis of its origi-nal character in his notes to lines 1330-39, p. 235. I see no point in distracting a modern audience with a fairy story that has nothing to do with the essence of this masterful play, and would advise a modern director to leave these lines out.

the passions of mere men.
DIONYSUS. My father sanctioned this
   in ages past: great Zeus.
AGAVE. [*rising forlornly from her knees*]
   Old man, it is decreed.
   Our sentence is complete:
      our fatal banishment. 1350
DIONYSUS. Then why do you delay
   what cannot be undone?
   [DIONYSUS *vanishes, and his voice echoes round the hills*]
CADMUS. [*turning with gentleness towards* AGAVE]
   My daughter, how we've fallen:
      to what a pass we've come!
   You and your poor sisters
      and I the wretched one:
   An old man as an alien,
      his home in alien lands.
   Then the sad prediction 1355
      that he must lead barbarian
   Mongrel hordes upon
      Hellas—he a serpent:
   Vicious as a snake:
   My wife a serpent also:
      Ares' child Harmonia
      [*turns to go*]
   So I am to lead her—
      lead her with my army
   Armed to raze the altars
      and sepulchres of Greece.
   Cadmus full of sorrows 1360
      shall find no respite ever.
   Even in the dungeon
      river-deeps of Acheron[7]
   He shall find no quiet.
AGAVE. [*clasping his knees and halting him*]
   O father, without *you* my exile will be sterile.
CADMUS. And so you throw your arms
      around me, my poor child:
   You a white-downed cygnet, 1365
      and I an ancient swan.[8]
AGAVE. Where then shall I turn,

---

7. *Acheron*: a river in Hades. Later gave its name to a department of Hades.
8. Many editors and translators, including Professor Dodds—*salva revenentia*—(but not Moses Hadas) seem to me not entirely to have hit the point here. The point is that Cadmus' reply to Agáve is ironic. She is thinking not so much of her father's plight as of her own, which her next remarks prove. Cadmus says, in effect, "If you are throwing your arms around me to protect *me* (like the proverbial swan protecting its decrepit sire), *you* are only a white-downed cygnet. . . . If you are throwing your arms around me to receive protection, I am only a useless old swan." Grammatically I do not see how line 1356 can be construed to translate, "As the young swan shelters the old, grown hoary and helpless" (Professor Dodds).

cast out from my home?
CADMUS. [*gently disengaging her*]
   I do not know, my daughter:
   your father is no help.

Envoi

[*The women of the* CHORUS *and the women of the maen-
adic group from the mountains begin to get into their for-
mations for the envoi as the music of flute, tambourine, cas-
tanet, and drum swells to* mezzoforte. AGAVE *and* CADMUS,
*in a slow, melancholy movement, walk toward the gates of
the city, holding a last elegiac conversation*]

AGAVE. Goodbye to my house, goodbye to my city:
   I leave you for exile to flee from my bridal home.   1370
   I leave you for misery.
CADMUS. Go now, my daughter, to Aristaéus . . .[9]
AGAVE. I weep for you, Father.
CADMUS. And I weep for you:
   Tears for yourself and tears for your sisters.
AGAVE. Because of a brutally ruthless fate
   Lord Dionysus visited on you—   1375
   Your house and your line.
DIONYSUS. [*his voice echoing from Mount Cíthaeron*] Yes, because
   of the ruthless way
   You dishonored his name in Thebes
      [AGAVE *and* CADMUS *halt and embrace*]
AGAVE. Father, farewell.
CADMUS.   Sad Daughter, farewell:
   A "well" that never will be.   1380
AGAVE. [*joined by a group of* MAENADS *she walks slowly toward the
   open country*]
   Escort me, my friends, to my pitiful sisters:
   To where I shall find those comrades in exile.
      I want to go far
   From the horrible eyes of butchery Cíthaeron—
   Far from my own vision of Cíthaeron   1385
   To a place no ghost of a thyrsus haunts . . .
      Let others meddle with bacchants.
      [*exit* AGAVE *into the distance*]
CHORUS. [*in a rhythmic march from the arena*][1]
   Many the forms of divine intervention:
   Many surprises are wrought by the gods.
   What was awaited was never created,   1390
   What was ignored, God found a way to.
      Such is this story today.
      [*exeunt* CHORUS, *followed last of all by* CADMUS]

9. "The sentence is incomplete and its
meaning unknown" (Dodds). Aristaeus
was husband of Autonöé and father of
Actáeon. Possibly she is to go to his
house in Thebes, and there with her sisters prepare for exile.

1. A modern director would no doubt
bring his curtain down after Agáve's
exit. A Greek dramatist (there being no
curtain) had to get his chorus out of the
orchestra.